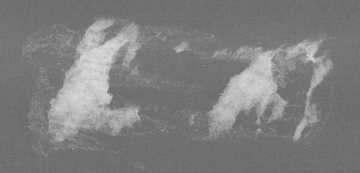

9128

*To our incredible, loyal and loving family and friends who helped shape this book, and to you, our readers – may you all eat like the kings and queens you are!*

# BEHIND
# the HALF
# DOOR

## stories of food and folk

Design, food styling and photography by Kady O Connell

# CONTENTS

*From reek of the smoke*
*And cold of the floor*
*And the peering of things*
*Across the half-door*

*Padraic Colum ~ A Cradle Song*

Sometime in 1875, a local fisherman built a hardy cottage beside the harbour on Coliemore Road in Dalkey, Ireland. On stormy days, when I battle to pull open the half door of this cottage, now my home, I think of him and the family that he perhaps had here and I, too, can feel the same sea salt on my mouth and on the wet webbed hair across my face.

My door was made in Donegal where my father's people came from. When I bought the cottage back in 1998, Da asked me to fold my arms in the hollow doorway while he measured me from foot to elbow with a piece of old string. The string would provide, for the Donegal carpenter, my exact measurements while leaning over a half door, and the height required for chatty comfort.

It is an ingenious Irish device, the half door. Its original purpose was to keep the animals out and the children in. A lady I know, ordinarily shy and somewhat reserved, recently quipped after drinking a large glass of Grüner Veltliner wine, "Ah, the half door.. it kept the hens in and the cocks out!" She grew red with laughter, as I topped her up.

The cottage's quaint, shy charm is a bit of a curiosity in Dalkey. It remains a small, proud, almost forgotten specimen of rural Ireland among the surplus electric-gated mansions and worn out housekeepers trudging back and forth. I wouldn't swap it for the world.

On a good day when the sea is calm, the smell of treacle bread and turf drift from my tiny kitchen across the half door, teasing locals and visitors to Dalkey. The aroma is irresistible, if I may say so myself – a heady, earthy, salty-sweet scent driving them all crazy. However, if you happen to peer through the half door, chances are you might see Kady and I silently measuring flour, nodding in agreement or tut tutting about the diversity of grains and butter. Yes, you would see two 'wimin' who like to cook with a curious eye on the past and a dewy cyclops' eye on the future.

Our book is an eclectic mix of recipes, folklore and interviews with renowned foodies through the ages, from boxer, George Foreman, to Michael Hartnett, a beloved poet, cook and friend.

We very much hope you will enjoy it.

Biddy and Kady xx

# *a bit about* Biddy

Since I was a mere crumb of a child, I have been fascinated by food, its provenance, its taste, its look, its history, folklore, superstition and heritage.

I have always felt that the constant patching and interweaving of food throughout history has marked our gift for survival; it has infected our humour, borne our resilience and marked us individually. How could it not.

While our petites French cousins in the 1840s were perfecting Bearnaise sauce and tackling towering confections of sugar, a sick, rampant famine meant that we Irish were forced to eat grass, charlock (a form of wild spinach) and stinking blighted black potatoes on the side of the road. Such paucity of ingredients, however, brought the unimaginable to the table.

The question visitors to my cottage in Dalkey most often asked, is: "Why did so many Irish people die of starvation when they were surrounded by a sea full of fish?" I asked Críostóir MacCárthaigh, archivist in the Irish folklore Department in UCD, this same question and his response was unhesitating. "There were always fish markets in Irish society, but when the famine came, there was less money to purchase fish and fishermen had to hock their nets, then their boats, for food. Then they became too weak to go out and collect fish."

Had we the same ancestral hunger pangs in 2017 gnawing through our stomachs, we would have eaten exactly what they had to. "Folklore about the Great Famine is rife with mentions of famine foods, familiar and unfamiliar – the list includes sycamore seeds, watercress, horse meat, dog meat, dog soup, laurel berries, red clover, heather blossoms, dandelions, nettles, donkey's milk, silverweed, goose grass, and much else."* Who knew – now our hippest foragers, bloggers and vloggers are greedily traipsing through hill and hillock in search of famine food.

My grand-uncle Edward Kearney (who married for the second time in his seventies) from Urrismanagh in County Donegal, was known, post famine, to be fond of an aul hedgehog. The dead animal would be rolled in wet muddy clay and when dry, it was put to roast on the turf fire. Once the clay began to crack, the hedgehog was removed from the fire and liberated from its sarcophagus, its needles pulled away with the clay to reveal white chicken like flesh.

A hedgehog a day keeps the doctor away?

When Kady and I travelled down to the country and mentioned recipes for pike or eels, many locals pulled faces, aghast at the mere thought of eating such things, a reaction even they agree, may have its roots in early famine times when poverty forced us to eat what was viewed as unpalatable at that time.

---

*Even today, there is an almost unconscious genetic shame connected to certain foods like pike, mussels, mackerel and eel. Through the worst atrocities, endured through us.*

*Poirteir 1995 61-64; 1996 31-39, 46,*

---

After working as a journalist for 20 years, it is an honour to share some of my favourite food stories along with all of my recipes in this book.

Le Grà,

Biddy xx

* 'R.N. Salaman, *The History & Social uses of the Potato (1949)*, Ch-15. Page 11.

# *a bit about* Kady

The best things in life start with the letter F. Family, friends and of course, my true love – food. For some people, it's sports or shoes; but food is my not-so-secret obsession. My friends fondly call me the muck savage and my fiancé knows he'll come second to a sandwich any day! If I'm not cooking it, I'm eating it, if I'm not eating it, I'm researching new recipes, or I'm helping clients with food photography and styling.

Originally from Limerick, I moved to Sydney in 2012 to pursue my creative dreams. It's here I found myself discovering the foodie scene and where I met and worked with some of the top food bloggers and authors, doing everything from food photography to recipe development.

With ignited passions and purpose; I realised this is what I was made to do. I made the terrifying and exhilarating decision to start my own business, Kady Creative, and have never looked back. Here I was designing cookbooks and doing branding for my favourite foodies and using my food blog, Kady's Kitchen, to share recipes and host pop-up dinners around Sydney.

My life revolved around food, and in a twist of fate; I found myself travelling and eating my way from country to country for 7 months. Who knew, after 4 years abroad, and months travelling; it would be back home in the small village of Dalkey, that I would meet my food soul-mate, Biddy.

I always dreamed of writing a cookbook, but never thought it would come true until this chance meeting. Biddy is your typical Irish Biddy – she drinks copious amounts of tea, lives in a cottage and is obsessed with food and Irish folklore. We connected instantly and, within hours, we were laying out the book and deciding on recipes.

Food has a special way of bringing people together. It's how we celebrate, comfort and create new memories. This book is a dream come true and something I never thought could happen. I feel so lucky to have met all of the incredible friends I have on this journey and to have the freedom to work for myself and pursue my passions.

I am so grateful to share this with you and hope from the bottom of my heart you enjoy it!

With love,

Kady xx

*foodie adventures @kadyskitchen*

BREAK

EAST + BRUNCH

# SMASHED AVOCADO
## *with* FETA + MINT

*serves* 2

It's so simple to make, but the fresh flavours in this breakfast truly sing. I think it's the dish that is most requested of me by my friends, and I know why – the smooth, creamy avocado tastes amazing with the sharp goat's feta and fresh sourdough. I whip this together nearly every morning, savouring it on my sunny Bondi balcony before I leave the house. You can swap in regular feta if you like, though goat's feta is easier to digest.

*1 large avocado*

*juice of ½ lemon*

*40g marinated goat's feta, drained and crumbled*

*1 tablespoon finely chopped mint leaves*

*2 slices sourdough bread*

*sea salt flakes, to taste*

Using a sharp knife, carefully cut the avocado in half lengthways and remove the stone. Score the flesh diagonally into 1cm squares. Using a spoon, scoop the cubes of avocado from their skin into a medium bowl.

Add the lemon juice and, using a fork, mash until smooth and combined. Add the feta and mint and gently stir to combine.

Spread each slice of the sourdough with the avocado smash. Sprinkle with a little sea salt to serve.

# OAT +
# BANANA PANCAKES

*serves* 2

The smell of oats always takes me back to my childhood – for me it conjures up memories of cosy breakfasts on chilly mornings in the Clare countryside, before a big day of mucking out the horses. My days in Bondi don't call for such sustenance now, but I still love the grounding, nourishing quality of oats, and often include them where I can. Case in point – my Sunday morning special – these guilt-free golden pancakes.

½ banana

⅓ cup (80ml) milk

1 cup (100g) rolled oats, processed until fine

1–2 drops vanilla extract

1 egg

1 pinch sea salt flakes

2 tablespoons butter

stewed berries or rhubarb (see recipe, page 184), to serve

mint leaves, to serve

Place the banana in a medium bowl and mash until smooth. Add the milk, oats, vanilla, egg and salt and mix until well combined.

Melt half the butter in a non-stick frying pan over medium heat. Cook the pancakes, in batches, for 3 minutes each side or until golden brown, adding more butter to the pan as necessary.

Stack and serve warm, topped with the stewed berries and mint.

# MIX 'n' MATCH
## *nutty* GRANOLA

*serves* 4

A little bit of crunch, some chewiness, a hint of sugar and a pinch of spice – the best part about this granola is mixing and matching whatever fruit and nuts you have on-hand! Don't be afraid to use this recipe as a base and get creative. Keep your granola sealed in a jar and come morning, spoon some into a bowl with natural yoghurt and fruit, or our stewed rhubarb (see *recipe*, page 184) – a delicious way to start the day!

*1 cup (100g) rolled oats*

*1½ cups (270g) quinoa*

*1 cup (110g) walnuts, coarsely chopped*

*½ cup (65g) dried cranberries*

*½ cup (100g) dried figs, coarsely chopped*

*½ cup (65g) sunflower seeds*

*½ cup (40g) flaked almonds*

*1 tablespoon flaxseeds*

*1 teaspoon ground cinnamon*

*¼ cup (20g) shredded coconut (optional)*

*2 tablespoons coconut oil, melted*

*¼ cup (60ml) maple syrup*

*½ teaspoon vanilla extract*

Preheat oven to 180°C (350°F). Line a baking tray with non-stick baking paper and set aside.

Place the dry ingredients in a large bowl and mix. Place the coconut oil, maple syrup and vanilla in a small bowl and stir to combine. Add the maple mixture to the dry ingredients and mix until well combined.

Spread the granola evenly on the prepared tray and bake for 20 minutes or until golden and crisp.

# *cheesy* MOLTEN MUSHROOMS

*serves* 2

Mushrooms are a polarising vegetable like no other! In our household, there was no grey area, you either loved them or hated them. I was very firmly on 'team love' in this debate. As far as I'm concerned, if you combine their earthy, complex flavours with some creamy blue cheese and a little garlic, you're in pure mushroom heaven! I hope you'll agree.

*2 teaspoons ghee or butter*

*2 cloves garlic, crushed*

*½ small brown onion, finely chopped*

*3 cups (250g) mixed mushrooms, sliced*

*30g blue cheese, crumbled*

*1 tablespoon milk*

*sea salt & cracked black pepper, to taste*

*toasted soda or sourdough bread, to serve*

*flat-leaf parsley sprigs, to serve*

Heat half the ghee in a medium saucepan over low heat. Add the garlic and onion and cover with a tight-fitting lid. Cook, stirring occasionally for 10–15 minutes or until translucent and soft.

Heat the remaining ghee in a medium non-stick frying pan over high heat. Add the mushrooms and sauté for 10 minutes or until the mushrooms are soft and have darkened in colour. Transfer the mushrooms to the pan with the onion and garlic. Add the cheese and milk and stir until creamy. Season with salt and pepper and serve with the toast and parsley.

---

NOTE – Ghee is a clarified butter that originated in India. It has a high smoke point so is often easier to cook with than regular butter, which can burn. It still has a subtle buttery flavour. You can find it in most health food stores or delis. Butter can be used as a substitute but if the recipe calls for high heat, remember to add a little extra virgin olive oil into the pan with it.

---

# VELVETY EGGS *with* PEAS + PARMESAN

*serves* 2

I'm most definitely a breakfast person – I need to begin my day with something super nourishing. It's a ritual I love, savouring every last bite. This recipe is, in-part, inspired by having Iggy's, an amazing sourdough bakery, just down the road from me. I'm always thinking up new ways to use their heavenly bread. I think this creamy egg and pesto creation, with sweet fresh peas and bitey parmesan, does it justice.

*4 free range eggs*

*1 tablespoon milk (I use coconut or almond milk)*

*¼ cup (30g) frozen peas*

*sea salt & cracked black pepper, to taste*

*1 teaspoon ghee or butter*

*2 slices sourdough, toasted*

*1 tablespoon good-quality store-bought basil pesto*

*1 tablespoon finely grated parmesan*

*basil leaves, to serve*

Place the eggs, milk, peas, salt and pepper in a medium bowl and whisk to combine.

Melt the ghee in a medium non-stick frying pan over medium heat. Add the egg mixture, reduce the heat to low and cook, stirring gently, for 3–4 minutes or until just set but not dry (slow cooking is the key to creamy eggs).

Spread each slice of toast with the pesto. Place onto serving plates and top with the egg. Sprinkle with the parmesan and basil leaves to serve.

TIP – I always look for basil pesto that has been made with extra virgin olive oil, as opposed to vegetable oils. You can really taste the difference in quality, so be sure to read the jar's ingredients before adding it to your trolley.

# ROSEMARY, RICOTTA +
# *honeycomb* HOTCAKES

*makes 8–10*

This breakfast is a firm weekend favourite in my house. Think warm fluffy pancakes, puffed up by light and creamy ricotta, then topped with fresh raw honey and rosemary. It tastes like Christmas Day.

Find fresh ricotta at the deli section of your supermarket and honeycomb from health food stores and providores.

1¼ cups (300g) fresh ricotta

⅔ cup (160ml) milk

4 eggs, separated

1 cup (150g) plain (all-purpose) flour

1 teaspoon baking powder

1 pinch sea salt flakes

2 tablespoons butter

fresh honeycomb, to serve

2 sprigs rosemary, leaves picked

Place the ricotta, milk and egg yolks in a large bowl and mix to combine. Sift in the flour, baking powder and salt.

Place the egg whites in a medium bowl and, using an electric mixer, whisk until stiff peaks form. Add the egg white to the ricotta mixture in two batches and fold gently using a metal spoon.

Melt half the butter in a medium non-stick frying pan over medium heat. Add ¼ cup (60ml) of the batter to the pan and cook for 3–4 minutes each side or until golden. Repeat with the remaining batter, adding more butter to the pan as necessary. Stack and serve the hotcakes warm, topped with the honeycomb and rosemary leaves.

2391218

# crispy CRAB CAKES with SOFT-POACHED EGGS

*serves* 4

I was introduced to this dish when living in Vancouver (and discovering for the first time what brunch was!) As a 19-year-old from Limerick, my taste buds hadn't experienced anything like it – I remember like it was yesterday. The fresh, succulent crab meat, bursting with its signature sweetness, is fried into a crispy golden base that's simply asking for a poached egg – it's a must-try (and great for entertaining). Fresh crab meat is available from your local fishmonger, or buy it frozen from major supermarkets.

### CRISPY CRAB CAKES

460g crab meat

1 tablespoon whole-egg mayonnaise

1 teaspoon dijon mustard

2 spring onions (scallions), trimmed and finely chopped

1 egg

½ cup (60g) almond meal (ground almonds)

juice of ¼ lemon

½ teaspoon finely grated lemon rind

sea salt & cracked black pepper, to taste

2 tablespoons extra virgin olive oil

1 teaspoon white vinegar

4 eggs

finely chopped flat-leaf parsley leaves, to serve

To make the crispy crab cakes, place the crab meat, mayonnaise, mustard, onion, egg, almond meal, lemon juice and rind in a large bowl. Season with salt and pepper and mix well to combine. Refrigerate for 30 minutes. Using clean hands, divide and shape the mixture into 4 patties. Heat half the oil in a medium non-stick frying pan over medium heat. In two batches, fry the patties for 4 minutes each side or until golden and cooked through, adding more oil to the pan as necessary. Set aside and keep warm.

While the crab cakes are cooking, bring a medium saucepan of water to the boil over high heat. Reduce the heat to medium and add the vinegar. Using a spoon, gently swirl the water to create a whirlpool effect. Add 1 of the eggs to the middle of the whirlpool, allowing the water to shape the egg. Simmer for 2 minutes or until the white is opaque and the yolk feels just firm to the touch. Remove with a slotted spoon and drain on paper towel. Repeat with the remaining eggs.

Divide the crab cakes between serving plates and top with a poached egg. Sprinkle with parsley to serve.

A COTTAGE, A BOAT & A PIKE

a cottage, a boat & a

# PIKE

*"My God, it's a pike," we said in unison as Mark hauled the legendary scavenger into the boat. Everyone was in high spirits. We accomplished our mission...*

FIRST BREWED 1886 · H.PIKE & CO

PIKES BEER COMPANY

TRADE MARK
PIKE BRAND
REGISTERED

SPARKLING ALE

CLARE VALLEY
SOUTH AUSTRALIA.

BREWED FROM BEST MATERIALS ONLY.

Mention the word 'pike' in Ireland, and an array of understandings and opinions swell. Is it that dainty lethal weapon used by our soldiers in 1798 against the English? Is it a turn in the road leading nowhere? Or perhaps, worst of all - is it 'that' fish?

How many fish do you know that can floor a rat? That, in essence, is how we think of our indigenous pike – rat wrestlers. Ask a fish-eating Irish person if they have tried pike, and the natural reaction is something akin to stepping on a dirty nappy... in your bare feet... a winced, pinched face staring back at you at the mere mention of the poor predator.

How on earth could we eat such a 'dirty' scavenger? There are many horrendous tales, dark, mysterious stories and legends about pike. Lough Derg had the reputation of harbouring monster pike and in the 1800s it was reported in a local newspaper that pike, 'ugly aliens' as big as 90 and 92 pounds (42 and 41kg) in weight, were caught there and in Meelick on the River Shannon. Pike has always had a bad reputation here, but not so for our German, French, Dutch and Eastern European cousins who relish its bony corpse with quivering excitement.

About 20 years ago, I was invited by friends to the uber chic "Voltaire" restaurant in Paris for lunch. I ordered 'a culinary jewel' from the Rhone-Alps region of France called 'Quenelle de brochet'. When said jewel arrived, I admired its aspect before delicately tasting and then quickly scoffing the two oval shaped frothy mousses presented on my plate. I discovered it to be a refined, rich, subtle delight served with a creamy Nantua sauce (a classical French fish sauce consisting of Béchamel, cream, crayfish butter and crayfish tails). The dish was definitely high on the cholesterol sphere with tons of cream, butter and fat, and yet it felt incredibly light in the tummy. "What," I asked our dear waiter, "have I just eaten?" It was just so incredibly… amazingly, wonderfully, good – and his reply was, "Mais, brochet, bien sur Mademoiselle."

*Brochet ~ definition ~ sing. pike; pl. pike*

*Quelle horreur*, I ate pike! Should I wash my mouth out? *Non, mes amis*, do not le mouth wash out. It was truly one of the finest fish dishes I had eaten in years and I still, to this day, think about it.

By God, the French have found an ingenious way of tackling this energetic predator – sieve him. (Le chef at 'Voltaire' explained that this pike dish required precise techniques and knowledge of poached pike forcemeat in order to achieve the exquisite result on my plate.)

So now, we arrive in Longford, Kady and I, on our odyssey for pike. Our first day we spend with Michael Masterson, a remarkable man; storyteller, stone mason and folklorist who had undertaken to take us on a peek-a-boo of the old pike, its ways and habitat.

Firstly, he introduced us to two grand buckos, 'the Deputy' (John Kenny) and local fisherman and accomplished chef, Mark Nicholls – both walking examples of that old adage, "easy come, easy go." Kady and I were going pike fishing.

I remember it now as an unforgettable day. A stiff breeze was blowing as we arrived on the edge of Lough Tully with Michael and 'the Deputy', who was wearing green wellies up to his oxters. 'The Deputy' assisted us to the boat, bursting with pride as he helped the 'two blondes'. "The ground is marshy and muddy, so Michael will jockey-back the both of ye into the boat," he said with a reassuring pat. Mark was waiting for us. Letting the boat drift, he attached his copper spoon bait to a 25-pound line and a float about 3-foot in length, and then he told us of his many encounters with pike. "It's an ugly fish. People don't eat pike because they say they eat rats, but if you get them at 3 pounds weight when they are

young and before they start scavenging, they are delicious." He rowed gently near the shallow margins of the lake. "The biggest one I ever caught was 20 pounds in weight and that was twenty years ago – and that fella was tame. I always fish around the shore of the lake, the pike feed around the dock leaves."

Suddenly, there was a desperate tug which nearly pulled the rod from Mark's hand and almost knocked the two lads out of the boat. A battle had begun. With all the impending excitement, I thought of George's battle with the dragon and I must say, Mark's wasn't any less impressive. The pike wasn't a whopper, but substantial all the same.

We returned to Mark's house where we heard stories of its sedgy life under water like how pike hunt roach and trout in the dark crevices of the lake.

"The bones of the pike were called 'the thorn', he said, as we all peered closer inspecting the warrior on the wooden table. "It's like eating cotton wool with needles," cried 'the Deputy'.

"Yep, 'the Deputy's' right," said Mark cleaning our 3-pound friend. "The filleted bones run parallel through the body of the fish as well as across it like normal fish bones. You have to eat it carefully with your fingers, constantly picking at it. That's why people don't serve it that much. No matter how careful you eat it, there is always a lethal bone sticking out." (Please note sieve method above).

"My mother, Carmel Nicholl from Aughava, used to cook thin slices of it. She never put flour on pike as it made it look like any other fish. When you cook it without flour, in the old fashioned traditional way, it is much more beautiful. You can see the scales and the colours of its skin. Nowadays, recipes cover everything up," he said, as he respectfully placed a line of lemon slices inside its hollow body – a balm to marinate its flesh.

"Bake it slow with some olive oil, not rapeseed oil, it's too strong and taints the taste." While we waited, Mark plied us with long, cool glasses of St Mel's Pale Ale, a local treat. Guess what, the pike wasn't half-bad either. Kady and I still talk about our trip to Longford and how indebted we are to the lads for their kindness. À *bientôt* – next stop Leitrim, for good old Boxty.

A jockey-back for Biddy (left);
Mark's gleaming pike (right).

ISH + SEAFOOD

# creamy HALIBUT with PEAS, PISTACHIO + MINT

*serves 2*

A simple and warming dinner idea, this meal invokes seaside memories for me. I first tried the earthy flavour combination at a Taste of Sydney event and knew I would need to try to re-create it. The pistachios add a lovely crunch to the silky smooth mash and sweet baby peas. I love the delicate flavour of halibut, but it can be tricky to find in some areas – you can use your favourite firm white fish in its place. Barramundi is a great alternative.

*300g skinless halibut fillets or your choice of firm white fish fillets*

*¾ cup (180ml) milk*

*sea salt & cracked black pepper, to taste*

*2 medium potatoes (400g), peeled and diced*

*1 tablespoon butter*

*2 tablespoons single (pouring) cream*

*1⅓ cups (160g) frozen peas, cooked*

*2 tablespoons shelled pistachios, coarsely chopped*

*2 tablespoons mint leaves*

Place the fish and milk in a small saucepan and bring to the boil over high heat. Reduce the heat to low, season with salt and pepper, cover with a tight-fitting lid and poach for 10–15 minutes or until cooked through. Drain and flake the fish, reserving the milk, and remove any small bones.

While the fish is poaching, place the potato in a saucepan of simmering water and cook for 15 minutes or until soft. Drain and return to the pan. Add the butter, cream and 1–2 tablespoons of the reserved poaching milk and mash until smooth and creamy. Add the fish and gently stir to combine. Season to taste.

Divide the creamy fish and peas between serving plates and top with the pistachio and mint.

# *FRIED MACKEREL* in oats with *bramley* APPLE + MINT SAUCE

*serves* 4

Every July and August my friend Catherine and I would go mackerel fishing in her little boat. Armed with hand lines, their pretty orange feathers blowing in the breeze, a sharp knife and a bucket, we would fish in the Dalkey Sound. It was so relaxing being at sea on a sunny day, rowing around the rugged beauty of Dalkey Island. The mackerel were plentiful at this time and often when we came across a shoal, they'd nearly jump into the boat. Their beautiful skins would gleam grey and silver, with a gorgeous rosy iridescence on the sides. Back in the cottage, a hank of mackerel in my bucket, I would cook them like my father used to. Here is the recipe.

*2 eggs*

*1 cup (100g) rolled oats*

*1 teaspoon sea salt flakes*

*1 teaspoon cracked black pepper*

*4 mackerel fillets, pin boned*

*2 tablespoons butter*

*bramley apple sauce with mint (see recipe, page 184), to serve*

Place the eggs in a medium shallow bowl and whisk. Place the oats, salt and pepper in a large shallow bowl and mix to combine. Pat 1 fillet of fish dry with paper towel and dip into the egg mixture. Press both sides into the oats to coat. Repeat with the remaining fillets.

Melt half the butter in a non-stick frying pan over medium heat. When the butter begins to foam, add half the fish and cook for 3 minutes each side or until golden, crisp and cooked through. Repeat with the remaining fish, adding more butter to the pan as necessary.

Divide between serving plates and top with the apple sauce to serve.

# OYSTERS *with* TOMATO + LAVENDER VINAIGRETTE

*serves* 4 *as a starter*

This zingy topping for salty sea oysters is sweet and sharp all at once.
The subtle notes of crushed lavender, tomato and shallot infuse the vinegar,
making for a simple yet impressive starter – just perfect for entertaining.

*4 cherry tomatoes, seeded and finely chopped*

*1 french shallot (eschalot), finely chopped*

*1 tablespoon crushed lavender buds*

*sea salt & cracked black pepper, to taste*

*¼ cup (60ml) white balsamic vinegar*

*12 freshly shucked oysters, in their shells*

Place the tomato, shallot, lavender, salt, pepper and vinegar in a small
bowl and whisk to combine. Refrigerate for 6–8 hours or overnight.

Arrange the oysters on a serving plate that's topped with crushed ice
(optional). Spoon the vinaigrette onto each oyster to serve.

*i need a holiday*

# POACHED SALMON

*serves 2*

Bondi is sunny and fabulous most of the year, but of course there are a couple of months when cold wind and rain prevail. These months seem to double as a really busy time for me, so I love to cook this dish as a little escape, imagining I'm somewhere tropical sipping piña coladas instead!

Infused with punchy Asian flavours and fresh young coconut, it's a little slice of island life in your very own kitchen.

*1 young coconut, opened*

*1 red onion*

*2 cloves garlic, peeled*

*1cm fresh ginger*

*1 tablespoon soy sauce*

*juice of 1 lime*

*2 x skinless salmon fillets*

*1 small red chilli, finely chopped (optional)*

*coriander (cilantro) leaves, to serve*

*shredded coconut, to serve*

Preheat oven to 180°C (350°F). Pour the coconut water into a small food processor. Using a flexible spatula or palette knife, carefully remove the white flesh from the inside of the coconut and add it to the processor. Add the onion, garlic, ginger, soy and lime juice and process until smooth.

Arrange the salmon fillets in a small baking dish. Top with the coconut mixture and bake for 15–20 minutes or until the salmon is cooked through.

Divide the salmon between serving plates and spoon over the hot coconut sauce. Sprinkle with the chilli, coriander and shredded coconut to serve.

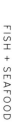

# SEARED MONKFISH *with* BLACKCURRANT BRAMBLE

*serves 4*

Years ago in Ireland people would startle at the idea of seeing, let alone eating, 'the monster' (aka monkfish). Its ugly face and sharp little teeth frightened them, unsurprisingly really considering the long association between monkfish and ghouls in Irish folklore. But in the kitchen, we know there's no need to fear this delicious fish – it's highly-prized and best cooked simply as it is here. If your fishmonger can't source it for you, it can be substituted with rock lobster.

*2 tablespoons ghee or butter*

*4 x 200g skinless monkfish fillets*

*4 sprigs samphire or rosemary*

*finely grated rind of 2 lemons*

*2 teaspoons sea salt flakes*

*blackcurrant bramble (see recipe, page 182)*

Preheat oven to 220°C (425°F). Melt the ghee in a large ovenproof frying pan over high heat. Pat the fish dry using paper towel and sprinkle with the samphire, lemon rind and salt.

Cook the fish for 2 minutes each side before transferring the pan to the oven. Roast for 6–8 minutes or until cooked through when tested.

Divide between serving plates and serve with the blackcurrant bramble.

# SEAFOOD STEW *with* MA'S *fluffy* DUMPLINGS

*serves 4*

This recipe is a 'thank you note' to my mother, Deirdre, for all her toil, baking and cooking for a family of seven girls and one boy. We were well-fed, that's for sure. There was a time in my youth when I couldn't get Ma's fluffy dumplings off my mind, even during a rare Irish heatwave! I can still remember those doughy balls, partly submerged in the salty simmering fish stew, expanding as they steamed (the secret is a light touch and ice-cold water). I'm afraid there is no season for comfort food! Fish stew is a classic dish but the addition of these dumplings takes it to a different level – try it for yourself!

2 tablespoons extra virgin olive oil

1 teaspoon butter

1 large onion, finely chopped

1 small leek, trimmed and finely chopped

4 cloves garlic, sliced

1 stalk celery, trimmed and chopped

½ fennel bulb, trimmed and finely chopped

½ teaspoon crushed fennel seeds

⅓ cup (80ml) dry white wine

1 bay leaf

600g canned chopped tomatoes

2 tablespoons tomato passata (purée)

finely grated rind of ½ orange

1 tablespoon chopped thyme leaves

2 teaspoons dried thyme leaves

2 teaspoons caster (superfine) sugar

¾ cup (180ml) good-quality fish or vegetable stock

a few drops of tabasco sauce

1 teaspoon tomato sauce (ketchup)

sea salt & cracked black pepper, to taste

1kg chopped mixed fish
(try smoked cod, salmon, hake and pollack)

1 tablespoon samphire or rosemary sprigs, to serve

### MA'S FLUFFY DUMPLINGS

⅔ cup (100g) self-raising (self-rising) flour

1 tablespoon baking powder

1 teaspoon dried mixed herbs

sea salt & cracked white pepper, to taste

55g frozen butter, grated

½ cup (125ml) ice cold water

Melt the oil and butter in a large heavy based saucepan over medium heat. Add the onion, leek and garlic. Cook, stirring, for 3–4 minutes or until soft. Add the celery, fennel and fennel seeds and cook for a further 3 minutes. Add the wine and bay leaf and cook for 1 minute. Add the tinned and pureed tomato, orange rind, thyme, sugar, stock, Tabasco and tomato sauce. Sprinkle with salt and pepper and bring to the boil. Allow to simmer for 20 minutes.

While the sauce is simmering, make the dumplings. Sift the flour and baking powder into a large bowl. Add the mixed herbs, salt and pepper. Mix to combine and add the butter. Using your fingertips, rub in the butter until the mixture resembles breadcrumbs. Gradually add the water and bring the mixture together to make a soft smooth dough, adding more water as necessary. Cut the dough into 4 pieces and, using floured hands, roll each piece into a ball.

Add the fish to the stew and stir to combine. Simmer for 5 minutes or until cooked through and opaque.

Add the dumplings, and cover with a tight-fitting lid. Simmer, undisturbed, for 10 minutes or until the dumplings have risen and are fluffy on the inside when tested with a fork.

Sprinkle with samphire to serve.

# MUSSELS *cooked in* CIDER *with* GARLIC BREAD

*serves* 2

In my mind, this is how mussels should be enjoyed – in the most simple way. This recipe came from my aunt, Marie, who is always giving me magazine clippings and photocopies of her favourite things to cook. (Now that I'm in Sydney I receive them in the post!) You could also try simmering mussels in white wine, but I love the sweet, earthy flavour of cider. Garlic is also a natural partner for mussels, and I'll often serve this dish with toasted sourdough that's laden with butter and a little crushed garlic.

*1 teaspoon coconut oil or butter*

*4 french shallots (eschalots), finely chopped*

*2 cloves garlic, finely chopped*

*1 cup (250ml) apple cider*

*1kg mussels, cleaned*

*⅓ cup (80ml) coconut milk (optional)*

*juice of 1 lime*

*2 tablespoons coriander (cilantro) leaves*

### CRUSTY GARLIC BREAD

*1 small clove garlic, crushed*

*1 tablespoon finely chopped flat-leaf parsley leaves*

*2 tablespoons butter, softened*

*2 thick slices sourdough or white soda bread (see recipe, page 169), toasted*

Melt the coconut oil in a large heavy-based saucepan over low heat. Add the shallot and garlic, cover with a tight-fitting lid and cook for 10 minutes or until soft.

Increase the heat to high and add the cider and mussels. Cover and allow to simmer for 5–7 minutes or until each mussel has opened. Add the coconut milk and stir until combined and warmed through.

To make the crusty garlic bread, place the garlic, parsley and butter in a small bowl. Mix well to combine and spread over the sourdough. Place the bread under a grill (broiler), preheated to high, for 2–3 minutes or until crisp and golden.

Divide the mussels between serving plates and top with the lime juice and coriander. Serve with the warm garlic bread.

# SCALLOP CEVICHE

*serves* 2 *as a starter*

This is a beautiful, zesty, summery dish. It's packed full of citrus flavour and it's really light. I once made it for a picnic we had on Dalkey Island. Biddy, my dad and my brother all headed over on the fisherman's boat to eat lunch in the sun. Packed chilled into our hamper, this ceviche was a big hit (and went down a treat with a glass of bubbly!).

*120g fresh scallops, quartered*

*juice of 1 lime*

*2 teaspoons lemon juice*

*2 cloves garlic, crushed*

*1 small red chilli, seeded and sliced*

*sea salt flakes, to taste*

*1 tablespoon coriander (cilantro) leaves, chopped*

Place all the ingredients in a medium bowl. Mix to combine and allow to marinate in the fridge for 2 hours or until chilled.

# HAMBURGERS & GOD

**M**any years ago, I was filled with a profound sense of pugilistic and culinary purpose and to that end I made up my mind to track down the world famous heavyweight boxer, George Foreman. Why? Because the veteran of the "Rumble in the Jungle" and Ali's biggest thorn, had not only one of the most flamboyant careers in boxing but boy, did he love his grub, just like me. I wanted to seek out 'Big George', the body behind the 'George Foreman Lean Mean Fat-Reducing Grilling Machine.*' I wanted to meet the "Punching Preacher," and pray with him in Humble, the aptly named suburb of Houston, Texas, where he resides to this day. But how could I leave on this adventure of a lifetime without my trusty travelling companion and little sister, Nibs – I couldn't.

## TEXAS

With the erudite sangfroid of a bad comedienne, OH, our taxi driver, mesmerised us with stories of George's obsession with food. "I reckon he eats 35 cheeseburgers a day," said OH nonchalantly.

Almost from the time of his birth on January 10th, 1949, hunger shaped Foreman's impoverished childhood in the Fifth Ward, Houston. He knew quite a bit about poverty. One of seven children, he lived it – his Father drank away most of his rail worker's salary and fought ferociously with his mother. They were always starving.

In the early seventies, he would become a church minister, but later, a junk-food addiction would take hold of him, ballooning him to over 300 pounds.

## HUMBLE, TEXAS. 1997

On a sticky Thursday morning, Nibs and I ran from our sickly pale yellow room in Houston's Ramada in search of George. We had no contacts for him, no address, no phone number. We used instinct and our big Irish noses to sniff him out and eventually we found George Foreman's house. It was a revelation. Simply gigantic. The gardener behind the huge iron gates measured about six foot seven. Does Mr Foreman live here? "Ye-as, he does," he said in a crawling southern drawl. He kindly told us where Foreman would be preaching later that night. "Why doncha boogie on down to the church hall, betcha ya'll meet him there." We thanked him and left.

As we walked away, Nibs placed her hand on a hip and took a deep breath. "Your horoscope says that courage and optimism are your best traits," she said swigging the day's fifth Diet Dr Pepper.

It was seven o'clock and a hot night in Texas when we found Foreman's church in Humble. There were only three cars outside Mr Foreman's church. Some locals aimlessly standing outside glanced at their watches. When we asked them did Mr. Foreman preach here, they whispered his name with the passion of a higher devotion and said "yes".

There was great excitement when the Punching Preacher arrived, and Nibs and I were popping with curiosity. Foreman strided purposefully through the main door, his huge frame blocking out all the light. We could hear him complaining about fruit drinks with alcohol. I had heard the Preacher is a 'dry' boy who only drinks milk, coffee and soda. "They didn't have those in my drinking days," he said to a young teenage boy.

"It's not the temptation, it's the living spirit that penetrates the human being," he said in biblical tones.

Nibs sized up his huge frame and his mood, and then stared at his Irishy tweed cap. We thought he would have preacher's clothes on, but he was dressed smartly in cream trousers, a brown shirt and a brown leather waistcoat. "He certainly looks well-fed," whispered Nibs. A child was crying as he walked towards the alter. "Somebody bawlin' with some baby," he said, sounding a touch cranky. Then he roared; "If my people's hearts are humbled or if my people shall humble themselves, then will I heal their land. Two Chronicles 7-14."

The Preacher casually sat down on the alter steps. He was surrounded by his sons, *George III, George IV, George V* and *George VI* and his daughter *Georgetta* who smiled at us broadly. Then the sermon started.

Every biblical reference was to food. As a child, he told his congregation, he had a constant hunger for hamburgers and a gnawing fear that he would starve. With that memory on board, he threw a large loping right that whizzed through the air towards the singers. Then one after another, the songs swelled out, 'Didn't my Lord deliver Daniel?', 'Ave Maria', then another and another. The sermon lasted more than an hour, with blood-curdling yells of reverent triumph

and wild cheers greeting Foreman's prayers for sick members of his community. It was lively.

When he had finished the sermon, his daughter-in-law introduced us to him. We were overawed – this was the man who destroyed Smokin' Joe Frazier 24 years ago and flattened Michael Moorer in 1994. But this was also the man who, by 1977, had four children by four different women, who drank and smoked himself into the gutter.

When he realised that we were from Ireland, he relaxed and spoke of Limerick. "I have never been to Ireland but I just read Frank McCourt's book, Angela's Ashes, it's a fine book, the poverty, oh the poverty. It's shameful."

"We lived mainly on nickles and dimes my mother made," he said. "Between the seven of us there was never enough food for me. A good breakfast was a bowl of cornflakes, some evaporated milk diluted with water and a little sugar. I'd dilute the remaining drops of milk, then hopelessly shake the sugar bowl to get out a few more grains. Every Sunday we'd get one strip of bacon each. On Fridays, she'd bring home a single hamburger and break it into eight pieces. Everybody got a taste. In school I lived on mayonnaise sandwiches."

Foreman recalled being clothed in used garments donated by the people at the restaurant his Mother worked at. "I stole goods, picked fights, drank. At that stage," he said smiling at Nibs, "religion seemed like hokum."

"I think I'll buy us some Buffalo fish and I'll fry it for George," said the Preacher's wife Joan, arriving to pick him up and already thinking of his favourite subject – food. My stomach rumbled just listening to her and they were off.

## HOUSTON

On a Delta flight from Houston to Atlanta Airport, Nibs and I smiled to ourselves. A single impulse had pointed us to George Foreman. The most peculiar things in life can be the most wonderful, I thought. We never imagined we would hear a sermon about quarter pounders, hickory smoked bacon and God. We never imagined we'd meet George Foreman in a little town called Humble. We could never imagine what it would be like to be hungry.

*Since its introduction in 1994, over 100 million George Foreman grills have been sold worldwide.*

M

EAT + POULTRY

# PEAR + PISTACHIO
## *stuffed* PORK

*serves 4–6*

The tender pork in this recipe is stuffed with all sorts of goodness (think pistachio, pear, spices, apricot and onion). Seared in butter, I love the warm salty smell as it roasts in the oven. It's a great winter lunch or dinner, served with hot apple sauce, but I also like it in summer too, sliced cold with a chilled glass of German riesling.

### PEAR AND PISTACHIO STUFFING

*2 tablespoons butter*

*2 teaspoons extra virgin olive oil*

*1 medium onion, finely chopped*

*8 cloves garlic, finely chopped*

*1 medium pear or apple (150g), peeled, cored and finely chopped*

*½ cup (75g) soft dried apricots, finely chopped*

*½ cup (90g) pistachios, finely chopped*

*1 teaspoon cumin seeds, crushed*

*1 teaspoon fennel seeds, crushed*

*2 large sage leaves*

*1 teaspoon thyme leaves*

*finely grated rind of 1 lemon*

*1½ cups (100g) fresh white breadcrumbs*

*1 teaspoon sea salt flakes*

*½ teaspoon cracked black pepper*

### PORK

*2 x 600g pork fillets (tenderloins)*

*juice of 1 lemon*

*sea salt & cracked black pepper, to taste*

*2 teaspoons butter*

*2 teaspoons extra virgin olive oil*

*pear or apple wedges, to serve*

*sage leaves, to serve*

To make the pear and pistachio stuffing, melt half the butter and half the oil in a large non-stick frying pan over low heat. Add the onion and garlic and cook, stirring frequently, for 2 minutes or until translucent. Transfer the onion mixture to a large bowl. Melt the remaining butter and oil in the pan. Increase the heat to medium and add the remaining ingredients. Cook, stirring, for 2–3 minutes or until combined and fragrant. Transfer to the bowl with the onion mixture, mix well to combine and allow to rest.

Preheat oven to 200°C (400°F). While the stuffing is resting, place the pork fillets on a flat surface. Using a sharp knife, slice each fillet lengthways, cutting only three-quarters of the way through. Butterfly the pork by pressing each side down and flattening to a 2cm thickness, using a meat mallet or rolling pin. Drizzle with the lemon juice and sprinkle with salt and pepper. Melt the butter and oil in a large non-stick frying pan over high heat. Add the pork and sear for 1–2 minutes each side or until golden brown. Remove from the pan and allow to rest.

To stuff the pork, top the centre of each fillet lengthways with the stuffing mixture. Fold the pork to enclose and secure with kitchen string. Place the pork in a large roasting dish and roast for 50 minutes–1 hour or until cooked through to an internal temperature of at least 63°C (145°F). Allow to rest for 5–10 minutes before slicing. Divide the pork between serving plates and serve with the pear and sage.

---

NOTE – Bramley apple sauce with mint (see *recipe*, page 184) is a delicious accompaniment to this dish.

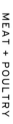

# PULLED HAM CROCK POT
## *with* PEAR SALAD

*serves* 4

This dish is easy and packed with flavour. For busy souls it's the ideal recipe, as you can simply throw everything into the slow cooker (crock pot) in the morning, turn it on and by the time you get home you have this delicious stringy, tender ham. Plate your salad and hey presto! I've discovered there's a knack to using a slow cooker. It helps to start on the 'high' setting for half an hour, just to bring the liquid up to temperature faster. Then cook on low for 7 hours, and never take the lid off during cooking – like an oven, heat escapes and it will take more time to return to the correct temperature. Enjoy!

*1 x 1.5kg ham fillet*

*1 cup (250ml) water*

*1 cup (250ml) good-quality red wine*

*1 teaspoon worcestershire sauce*

*1 large onion, chopped*

*4 cloves garlic, sliced*

*2 carrots, chopped*

*1 stalk celery, trimmed and chopped*

*6 black peppercorns*

*1 bay leaf*

*½ teaspoon caster (superfine) sugar*

**PEAR SALAD**

*2 ripe pears*

*16 whole cloves*

*1 tablespoon butter*

*½ cup (50g) walnuts*

*2 teaspoons caster (superfine) sugar*

*1 bunch (350g) watercress, tough stems trimmed*

*⅓ cup (80ml) sweetie sharpy salad dressing (see recipe, page 186)*

Place the ham in a 2-litre electric slow cooker. Add the water, wine and Worcestershire sauce. Add the onion, garlic, carrot, celery, peppercorns, bay leaf and sugar. Cover tightly with the lid.

Cook on high for 30 minutes. Reduce the heat to low and cook for a further 7 hours or until the ham is tender enough to shred. Drain the liquid, discarding the vegetables, and shred the meat.

To make the pear salad, peel, core and slice the pears into crescents. Press 1 clove through each segment. Place the butter in a medium heavy-based frying pan over medium heat and cook until gently bubbling. Add the pear and walnuts and sprinkle with the sugar. Cook, turning, for 2–3 minutes or until golden and caramelised.

In a large serving bowl, layer the watercress, pear and walnuts. Drizzle with the dressing and top with warm strips of ham. Serve warm.

# LAMB SHANKS *in* RIESLING

*serves 4–6*

The ultimate one-pot dinner, once you've mastered this hearty dish you'll feel equipped to feed an entire table of loved ones. I remember making this for some half-starved friends on one of the wettest, windiest nights in Dalkey. I emerged from the cottage kitchen to prolonged cheering, and then the empty plates were cleared to great applause. Warming, simple and rustic – it's a true crowd-pleaser. I like to use a heavy cast-iron casserole dish for this recipe. The riesling lends a flavourful but light touch and the long slow cooking means the lamb is as tender as can be.

¼ cup (60ml) extra virgin olive oil

4 x 450g lamb shanks, trimmed

1 large onion, finely chopped

8 cloves garlic, sliced

2 stalks celery, trimmed and chopped

4 carrots, peeled and chopped

1 bulb baby fennel, trimmed and finely sliced

1 bottle (750ml) good-quality dry riesling

1 cup (250ml) chicken or vegetable stock

6 dried apricots

1 bay leaf

4 sprigs rosemary

6 sprigs thyme

juice of ½ lemon

sea salt & cracked black pepper, to taste

boiled or mashed potatoes, to serve

finely chopped flat-leaf parsley, to serve

Preheat oven to 140°C (285°F). Heat the oil in a large heavy-based saucepan over medium heat. Add the lamb and cook for 3–4 minutes or until browned on all sides. Remove from the pan and set aside.

Add the onion, garlic, celery, carrot and fennel to the pan and cook, stirring, for 2–3 minutes or until the onion is soft. Return the lamb to the pan. Add the wine, stock, apricot, bay leaf, rosemary, thyme, lemon juice, salt and pepper. Stir to combine and bring to the boil. Cover with a tight-fitting lid and transfer to the oven. Cook for 3 hours or until the meat is just falling off the bone.

Remove any fat from the surface with a spoon and, if necessary, season with extra salt, pepper or lemon juice to taste. Divide between serving bowls with potatoes and sprinkle with parsley to serve.

# POACHED CHICKEN *in* TARRAGON BROTH *with* *caramelised* GRAPES

*serves* 4

This protein-packed dish is quick to prepare and super-tasty. It's warming and light, perfect for busy days or if you're feeling a little under the weather. Friends once valiantly advised me to thicken it up with a roux, but I must say I prefer it fresh and clear. In case you're in the mood for something richer, I've added directions for turning it into a creamy sauce. Everyone happy? I hope so.

2 tablespoons butter

4 x 150g chicken breast fillets

sea salt & cracked white pepper

2 cups (500ml) good-quality dry white wine

2½ cups (625ml) chicken stock

1 bay leaf

1 teaspoon finely chopped thyme leaves

2 tablespoons finely chopped tarragon

½ stalk celery, trimmed, outer skin peeled, chopped

1 cup (200g) green grapes

1 teaspoon caster (superfine) sugar

extra tarragon leaves, to serve

Grease a large heavy-based saucepan with half the butter. Sprinkle the chicken with salt and pepper and arrange in the pan, smooth-side up. Place over medium heat and top with the wine and stock. Add the bay leaf, thyme, tarragon, celery and half the grapes. Bring to a simmer, reduce the heat to low and cover with a tight-fitting lid. Poach for 15 minutes or until the chicken is cooked through.

While the chicken is poaching, melt the remaining butter in a small non-stick frying pan over medium heat. Halve the remaining grapes. Add the sugar and grapes, cut-side down. Cook, without turning, for 4–5 minutes or until caramelised and golden.

Divide the broth and chicken between serving bowls. Sprinkle with the caramelised grapes and extra tarragon to serve.

NOTE – Once the chicken is cooked through, you can remove it and reduce the liquid over medium heat to make a more flavourful broth, adding more seasoning if necessary. Alternatively, for a thicker, richer sauce, in a separate pan over medium heat, melt 2 tablespoons of butter until bubbling. Add 2 tablespoons plain (all-purpose) flour and cook, stirring, until a paste, or roux, forms. Gradually ladle the hot broth into the pan, whisking constantly, until fully combined. Cook for a further 5–7 minutes or until the sauce has thickened to your liking. Stir through 2 tablespoons double (thick) cream and divide between serving bowls with the chicken and grapes as above.

# *don't tell a porky* SPICED SCHNITZELS *with* RUSTIC APPLE + THYME SAUCE

*serves* 4

I first tried pork schnitzel in Sexton, Austria, where my two mischievous nephews live. They were unanimous in their adoration of this dish and I was quick to agree. It's easiest to ask your butcher to pound pork steaks into schnitzels for you, however I'll sometimes do it at home – just place the meat between sheets of baking paper and use a rolling pin to beat them (a great stress-reliever!) into lovely, thin schnitzels. This version is spicy, with a hint of jerk seasoning, and is coated in sourdough breadcrumbs. The apple and thyme sauce, though not traditional, is a perfect sweet companion for the pork.

**SPICE PASTE**

*juice of 1 lemon*

*⅓ cup (80ml) extra virgin olive oil*

*1 tablespoon water*

*2 tablespoons brown sugar*

*2 teaspoons sea salt flakes*

*1 teaspoon cracked black pepper*

*2 teaspoons thyme leaves*

*1 teaspoon dried thyme leaves*

*1 teaspoon ground cinnamon*

*2 teaspoons ground allspice*

*2 teaspoons ground cayenne pepper*

*¼ cup (65g) dried garlic granules*

*4 x 150g pork schnitzels*

*½ cup (75g) plain (all-purpose) flour*

*sea salt & cracked black pepper, to taste*

*2 eggs*

*¼ cup (60ml) milk*

*2 cups (200g) sourdough breadcrumbs*

*2 tablespoons coconut oil*

*rustic apple + thyme sauce
(see recipe, page 182), to serve*

To make the spice paste, place all the ingredients in a small food processor or blender and process into a paste.

Coat each schnitzel in the spice paste, place on a plate and refrigerate, covered, for 6–8 hours or overnight.

Allow the pork to return to room temperature. Place the flour, salt and pepper in a medium bowl and mix to combine. Place the eggs and milk in a separate medium bowl and whisk to combine. Place the breadcrumbs on a small shallow tray. Dust each schnitzel in the flour mixture, then dip into the egg mixture. Press each side of the schnitzels into the breadcrumbs to coat.

Heat half the oil in a large non-stick frying pan over high heat. Cook the pork, in batches, for 4 minutes each side or until golden and cooked through, adding more oil to the pan as necessary. Remove the schnitzels from the pan, drain on paper towel and keep warm. Divide between serving plates and serve with the apple sauce.

# biddy's COTTAGE PIE

*serves* 4

This is pure comfort food, warm and very tempting in the middle of a miserable Irish winter. There's always a whiff of nostalgia when I make this dish, for my mother's homely version which I have tried to reproduce for you here. I can still remember the joy of digging into her velvety mashed potatoes with crispy bits on top, the rich wine-infused meat and finely chopped vegetables. Enjoy this surrounded by family or friends when the rain is belting outside.

1 tablespoon extra virgin olive oil

1 teaspoon butter

1 medium onion, finely chopped

¼ leek, trimmed and finely chopped

2 carrots, finely chopped

450g beef mince

sea salt & cracked black pepper, to taste

2 cloves garlic, thinly sliced

1 teaspoon thyme leaves

1 tablespoon finely chopped flat-leaf parsley leaves, plus extra to serve

1 tablespoon plain (all-purpose) flour

1 tablespoon tomato paste

½ cup (125ml) good-quality red wine

1½ cups (375ml) beef or vegetable stock

2 tablespoons worcestershire sauce

1 tablespoon dark soy sauce

### CRISPY POTATO TOPPING

1kg floury potatoes, peeled and halved

sea salt flakes, to taste

2 tablespoons butter

¼ teaspoon white pepper

1 egg yolk

Heat the oil and butter in a large heavy-based saucepan over medium heat. Add the onion and cook, stirring, for 5–7 minutes or until just browned on the edges. Add the leek and carrot and cook for a further 5 minutes. Remove from the pan and set aside.

Increase the heat to high and add the beef. Cook, breaking up any lumps with a spoon, for 6–8 minutes or until well-browned. Sprinkle with salt and pepper and return the vegetables to the pan. Add the garlic, thyme and parsley and stir. Add the flour and stir, flattening any lumps with a spoon. Add the tomato paste and cook for 1 minute. Add the wine, stock, Worcestershire and soy, combine and bring to the boil. Reduce the heat to low, cover with a tight-fitting lid and simmer for 30 minutes.

Preheat oven to 200°C (400°F). Place the potato in a large saucepan, sprinkle with salt and cover with cold water. Place over medium heat and bring to the boil. Cook for 20–25 minutes or until tender when tested with a fork. Drain, return to the pan and cover with a tea towel to absorb the steam. Allow to stand for 5 minutes. Using a potato ricer or masher, mash the potatoes until smooth. Add the butter, pepper and egg yolk and mix well.

Transfer the beef mixture to a large baking dish. Spread the potato evenly over the beef, using the back of a spoon. Run the tines of a fork through the potato until the surface is rough. Place in the oven and cook for 20 minutes or until the potato is golden and crisp. Spoon into bowls and top with the extra parsley to serve.

NOTE – Chef Marco Pierre White always insists on really browning the meat for depth of flavour, and he is totally right. That extra bit of time involved is so worth it!

# grilled T-BONE STEAKS with
# MACERATED STRAWBERRIES

*serves 4*

It may seem like an unusual combination – a juicy grilled T-bone teamed with ripe strawberries and pretty pink peppercorns – but the taste sensation will stop you in your tracks. Sweet and sharp, with a delicious salty bite, this recipe is super easy to throw together and looks really impressive, too – try it for yourself.

*4 x 800g t-bone steaks, at room temperature*

*2 tablespoons extra virgin olive oil*

*1 tablespoon sea salt flakes*

*1 tablespoon pink peppercorns, crushed*

*1 tablespoon butter*

*⅓ cup (80ml) balsamic vinegar*

*⅓ cup (80ml) full-bodied red wine*

*1 teaspoon brown sugar*

*sea salt & cracked black pepper, extra, to taste*

*500g strawberries, halved*

Drizzle the steaks with the oil and sprinkle with the salt and pink pepper. Heat a heavy-based grill pan over high heat and cook the steaks for 5–6 minutes each side for medium rare or until cooked to your liking.

Remove the steaks from the pan and allow to rest for 5 minutes. Add the butter to the juices in the pan and top with the vinegar, wine, sugar and extra salt and pepper. Cook, stirring, until bubbling.

Add the strawberries and cook, mashing a few for extra flavour, for 4–5 minutes or until softened. Divide the steaks between serving plates and top with the strawberries and extra salt and pepper to serve.

# RIB EYE *and* TREACLE STEW

*serves* 4

The discussion around what cut of beef to use in a stew can become a little heated in my household. While some prefer chuck steak and others round, my personal favourite is rib eye. The lovely marbling of fat allows it to forge its own depth of character, making for rich, earthy flavours when cooked. It's also a quicker option for when time is of the essence but you still want a warming, tender beef stew. If I'm making this recipe for a special occasion, I'll often boil the potatoes separately so they're nice and white and fluffy upon serving.

*1 tablespoon extra virgin olive oil*

*2 tablespoons butter*

*450g rib eye steak, cut into 2cm cubes*

*sea salt & cracked black pepper, to taste*

*2 tablespoons plain (all-purpose) flour*

*1 tablespoon balsamic vinegar*

*1 small onion, chopped*

*6 pickled pearl onions, drained (optional)*

*6 cloves garlic*

*2 stalks celery, trimmed and roughly chopped*

*1 bay leaf*

*1 teaspoon chopped rosemary*

*4 sprigs thyme*

*1 bottle (750ml) good-quality red wine*

*1 litre beef stock*

*1 tablespoon dark soy sauce*

*1 tablespoon worcestershire sauce*

*2 tablespoons treacle (blackstrap molasses)*

*1 tablespoon demerara sugar*

*6 medium potatoes, peeled and chopped*

*4 carrots, roughly chopped*

*oregano leaves, to serve (optional)*

Preheat oven to 180°C (350°F). Heat the oil and half the butter in a large heavy-based saucepan over high heat. Add the beef and sprinkle with salt and pepper. Cook for 4–5 minutes or until the meat is browned on all sides. Add the flour and toss to combine. Add the vinegar and use it to help scrape any flour from the base of the pan. Transfer the meat and any juices to a heatproof bowl and set aside.

Melt the remaining butter in the pan and add the onion, pearl onions, garlic, celery, bay leaf and herbs and cook, stirring, for 3 minutes. Add the wine, stock, soy, Worcestershire, treacle and sugar. Stir to combine and bring to the boil. Skim the surface with a spoon to remove any unwanted oils or scraps. Cover with a tight-fitting lid, reduce the heat to medium and simmer for 10 minutes.

Return the meat and any juices to the pan and add the potato and carrots. Stir to combine, cover and transfer to the oven for 1 hour or until the meat is tender. Divide between serving bowls and top with the oregano to serve.

PASTA

*best-ever*

# LEMON SPAGHETTI

*serves 4*

Whenever I cook this unusual dish for supper in the cottage, everyone goes crazy for it. The sharp acidity of fresh lemon juice with sugar makes it sing. I shouldn't brag, but one of my Italian friends even took this recipe with him back to Verona (mind you, I don't think his mama was impressed – turmeric and pasta? Sacrilege!) Trust me, the addition of turmeric was purely accidental, and naturally there is a story behind it. When Kady was photographing this spaghetti one miserable morning in Dalkey, the dish looked particularly bland. Being an artist, I love colour, so I nipped into the kitchen, added turmeric, reheated the sauce and this golden delight was born.

¼ cup (60ml) extra virgin olive oil

1 tablespoon butter

1 onion, finely chopped

3 cloves garlic, finely chopped

3 teaspoons ground turmeric

1¾ cups (430ml) vegetable or chicken stock

3 teaspoons caster (superfine) sugar

2 cups (500ml) double (thick) cream

400g dried spaghetti

1 tablespoon thyme leaves

¼ x quantity crystallised lemon rind
(see recipe, page 186)

finely grated parmesan, to serve (optional)

Heat half the oil and all of the butter in a large frying pan over medium heat. Add the onion and garlic and cook, stirring, for 2–3 minutes or until translucent. Add the turmeric and stir to combine. Add the stock and sugar, bring to a simmer, reduce the heat to low and cook, stirring occasionally, for 10 minutes. Remove from the heat and allow to stand for 1 minute. Add the cream, folding gently into the sauce, and return to a low heat to warm through.

While the sauce is simmering, cook the pasta in a large saucepan of salted boiling water over medium heat for 8–10 minutes (or to packet instructions) until al dente. Drain, drizzle with the remaining oil and return to the pan.

Add the sauce to the hot spaghetti and toss gently to combine. Divide between serving bowls and top with the thyme, lemon rind and parmesan, to serve.

NOTE – Very few of us have time to spend crystallising lemon rind, however, I can assure you it's worth the effort for this dish (plus you'll have plenty leftover for later use) so I've included the recipe on page 186. You can, of course, use store-bought crystallised rind if you can find it at your local deli or gourmet food shop.

*creamy*

# AVOCADO PASTA

*serves 2*

I've always been obsessed with creamy pastas (let's face it, who isn't!).
They are just the ultimate comfort food. This velvety spaghetti is a bit different
and a little more virtuous than your average carbonara – it's actually the ripe
avocado that lends its creaminess. Combined with fresh buffalo mozzarella,
lemon and salt, it's a super-quick dinner solution for a cold rainy weeknight.

*200g spaghetti*

*1 large avocado*

*1 small clove garlic, crushed*

*juice of ½ lemon*

*sea salt flakes, to taste*

*1 tablespoon extra virgin olive oil*

*100g fresh buffalo mozzarella, drained and torn*

*8 cherry tomatoes, chopped (optional)*

*dried chilli flakes, to serve (optional)*

Cook the pasta in a large saucepan of salted boiling water over
medium heat for 8–10 minutes (or to packet instructions) until al dente.

Place the avocado, garlic and lemon juice in a medium
bowl and sprinkle with salt. Mash until smooth.

Drain the pasta and return to the hot pan. Add the oil and toss
to combine. Add the avocado mixture and toss gently to combine.
Add the mozzarella and tomato and fold through the pasta.

Divide between serving bowls and sprinkle with chilli flakes, to serve.

# MUSHROOM + NETTLE *risotto*

*serves 2*

Growing up, I would constantly be covered in nettle stings from running through the fields at my grandmother's house in Gillogue, County Clare. As it turns out, these ouchy little leaves are great to cook with (you just need to handle them with gloves before they hit the water). The addition of nettle to this tried and true mushroom favourite accentuates its warm earthy flavour and complements the goat's cheese perfectly (plus it's a great talking point when serving guests).

2 tablespoons nettle leaves

1 tablespoon butter

4 cloves garlic, finely chopped

1 medium brown onion, finely chopped

250g mixed mushrooms, roughly chopped

¾ cup (150g) arborio rice

½ cup (125ml) dry white wine

2 cups (500ml) vegetable stock, heated

60g goat's cheese

2 tablespoons lemon juice

sea salt & cracked black pepper, to taste

Wearing gloves, place the nettles in a medium heatproof bowl and cover with boiling water. Allow to stand for 30 seconds. Drain and set aside on paper towel (the nettles will lose their sting after they've been blanched).

Melt the butter in a large non-stick frying pan over low heat. Add the garlic and onion and cook, stirring, for 10 minutes or until translucent. Add the mushrooms and cook for 5–7 minutes or until soft. Add the rice and cook, stirring to coat in the butter, for 2–3 minutes before adding the wine. Once the wine has reduced a little, gradually add the stock, one ladle at a time, stirring continuously until it's absorbed before adding more. Cook for a further 10–15 minutes or until the rice is tender. Add the goat's cheese, nettles, lemon juice, salt and pepper and stir gently to combine. Divide between bowls to serve.

NOTE – Nettle leaves are best found wild and also make a delicious tea. As with anything found in the wild, be sure you know exactly what you're picking, or check with someone who does. Only use the leaves of nettles and be sure to blanch or dry them out so they lose their sting. Until then, handle them with gloves to avoid a nasty sting!

# VOLCANO of PASTA
## with SARDINES

*serves 4*

I first tasted pasta with sardines in Syracuse in Sicily. Admittedly I had indulged
in far too many glasses of Barolo and I was starving, but on repeated testing
I'm still adamant this dish is beyond good. It has that lovely mixture of salt and sea
that goes so well with pasta (and wine). If you don't feel like building a 'volcano'
you can always just eat the pasta and sauce as normal. Start preparing this
dish a day before eating, for maximum flavour and results – the sardines need
to marinate overnight, the sauce to cool completely and the pasta to then
shape into the volcano, before it erupts!

400g sardine fillets

½ cup (125ml) extra virgin olive oil

8 cloves garlic, finely chopped

¼ cup oregano leaves

juice of ½ lemon

sea salt & cracked black pepper, to taste

1 tablespoon butter

1 onion, finely chopped

½ bulb fennel, trimmed and finely chopped

½ cup (125ml) red wine

1⅔ cups (410ml) tomato passata (puree)

1¼ cups (310ml) fish or vegetable stock

2 teaspoons capers, rinsed and drained

1 tablespoon caster (superfine) sugar

2 tablespoons toasted pine nuts

450g spaghetti or bucatini

1 cup (70g) toasted breadcrumbs

finely grated parmesan, to serve

basil leaves, to serve

Place the sardines, overlapping slightly, in a large lightly greased baking dish. Drizzle with half the oil and
sprinkle with half the garlic. Top with the oregano, lemon juice, salt and pepper. Cover with plastic wrap
and refrigerate for 6 hours or overnight, to marinate.

Heat the remaining oil and the butter in a medium heavy-based saucepan over low heat. Add the onion,
fennel and the remaining garlic. Cook, stirring, for 5–7 minutes. Add the wine and cook for 3 minutes or until
reduced by half. Add the passata, stock, capers, sugar, pine nuts, salt and pepper and stir to combine.
Increase the heat to high and bring to the boil. Reduce the heat to medium and simmer for 10 minutes.
Allow to cool.

Preheat oven to 200°C (400°F).Pour the sauce over the sardines and bake for 25 minutes or until cooked
through and bubbling.

Cook the pasta in a large saucepan of salted boiling water over medium heat for 8–10 minutes (or to
packet instructions) until al dente. Drain in a colander, reserving 1 cup (250ml) of the cooking liquid if you
need to thin the pasta sauce, and place under cold running water to cool. Drain well.

Line the base and sides of a medium pudding or mixing bowl with half of the pasta, allowing strands to
overhang. Fill the bowl with a third of the sauce, then top with half of the remaining pasta. Repeat this step
and finish with the last layer of sauce. Cover this completely with the overhanging pasta. Cover with a sheet
of plastic wrap and a weight. Refrigerate for 6 hours or overnight.

Invert the bowl onto a serving plate and tap to release the pasta mound. Serve chilled, sprinkled with the
warm toasted breadcrumbs and topped with parmesan and basil leaves.

*succulent*

# CRAB LINGUINE

*serves 2*

I first made this dish in a cooking class back in Limerick. Over the years
I have tweaked it, but it's remained a staple in my recipe collection. It's one
of those classics that's so easy to make, yet seems kind of fancy and is great
for groups. I always make it when I have friends over so that I can be social
and leave the kitchen but we still get a delicious dinner – win win!

200g linguine or spaghetti

1 tablespoon extra virgin olive oil

1 brown onion, finely chopped

2 cloves garlic, crushed

1 yellow bell pepper (capsicum), finely chopped

2 tablespoons dry white wine

1 cup (250ml) single (pouring) cream

400g cooked crab meat

4–5 cherry tomatoes, sliced

2 tablespoons lemon juice

sea salt & cracked black pepper, to taste

2 tablespoons dill sprigs, to serve

finely grated parmesan, to serve

Cook the pasta in a large saucepan of salted boiling water over
medium heat for 8–10 minutes (or to packet instructions) until al dente.
Drain, reserving 1 cup (250ml) of the cooking liquid, and set aside.

Heat the oil in a large non-stick frying pan over medium heat. Add the
onion, garlic and capsicum and cook, stirring, for 5 minutes or until the
onion is soft. Add the wine and cook for 2–3 minutes or until reduced by half.
Add the cream, stir to combine and cook for 2 minutes or until thickened
slightly. Add the crab, tomato, lemon juice, salt, pepper and the reserved
cooking liquid. Stir and cook until heated through.

Divide between serving bowls and top with the dill and parmesan to serve.

# *creamy* CAULIFLOWER SPAGHETTI

*serves* 2

It's no secret cauliflower is the ultimate partner for cheese, but I often find its mild, fresh-but-cosy flavour is perfect with other rich foods, too – like in this comforting dish. Tossed with egg yolk, cream, pecorino and pasta, it's a little bit indulgent but a lot worth it.

*1 tablespoon extra virgin olive oil*

*1 medium head cauliflower (600g), cut into small florets*

*2 cloves garlic, finely chopped*

*sea salt & cracked black pepper, to taste*

*½ cup (125ml) single (pouring) cream*

*1 egg yolk*

*½ cup (40g) finely grated pecorino, plus extra to serve*

*200g spaghetti*

*8 anchovy fillets, finely chopped*

*1 tablespoon capers, rinsed and drained (optional)*

*rosemary sprigs, to serve*

Heat the oil in a medium non-stick frying pan over low heat. Add the cauliflower, garlic, salt and pepper and cook, stirring, for 10–12 minutes or until cooked through and golden.

Place the cream, egg yolk and pecorino in a medium bowl and whisk to combine.

Cook the pasta in a large saucepan of salted boiling water over medium heat for 8–10 minutes (or to packet instructions) until al dente. Drain, reserving ½ cup (125ml) of the cooking liquid.

Return the pasta to the pan and pour in the cream mixture and reserved cooking liquid. Place over low heat and cook, stirring, for 2–3 minutes or until slightly thickened. Divide between serving bowls and top with the cauliflower mixture, anchovy, capers, extra pecorino and rosemary to serve.

# roasted CAULIFLOWER and PARMESAN RISOTTO

*serves 4*

Some people shudder at the thought of making risotto, all that endless stirring and no guarantee it won't stick to the bottom of the saucepan. I really want to take that fear away. Once you know what to do, it's simple and really delicious. This ancient dish from Northern Italy is what I call sophisticated comfort food. Like all risotto, the rice is cooked in a broth until creamy, but the cauliflower is something a little different. Roasted with lemon zest and maple syrup, it's truly the perfect partner for rice.

### ROASTED CAULIFLOWER

*1 large cauliflower (800g), leaves trimmed*

*finely grated rind of 2 lemons*

*¼ cup (60ml) extra virgin olive oil*

*1 tablespoon maple syrup or honey*

*2 sage leaves, chopped*

*sea salt and cracked white pepper, to taste*

*2 tablespoons butter*

*1 tablespoon extra virgin olive oil*

*1 onion, finely chopped*

*2 cups (400g) arborio rice*

*1½ cups (375ml) dry white wine*

*1 litre vegetable or chicken stock*

*⅓ cup (55g) almonds*

*1 cup (80g) finely grated parmesan*

*thyme leaves, to serve*

To make the roasted cauliflower, preheat oven to 200°C (400°F). Cut the cauliflower in half and slice to remove the tough part of the core in a v-shape. Trim and discard any damaged or brown pieces. Break one half of the cauliflower into florets. Place in a medium bowl with the lemon rind, oil, maple syrup and sage and toss to combine (don't be tempted to add salt at this stage or it will not crisp). Spread out on a baking tray and roast for 10 minutes or until slightly charred on the edges. Sprinkle with the salt and pepper. Set aside to cool. Steam the remaining cauliflower until al dente.

Add the steamed cauliflower to a food processor with half the butter and process into a rough purée.

Place the oil and the remaining butter in a large heavy-based saucepan over medium heat. Add the onion and cook until translucent. Add the rice and cook, stirring to coat, for 2–3 minutes. Add the wine, a little bit at a time, stirring continually. Gradually add the stock, stirring between each addition until the liquid has been absorbed.

When the rice is tender, add the cauliflower purée, almonds and parmesan and stir until heated through and creamy.

Divide the risotto between serving bowls and top with the roasted cauliflower. Sprinkle with thyme leaves to serve.

# michael hartnett

(18 September 1941 – 13 October 1999).
An acclaimed Limerick poet.

On a windy day on October 15th 1999, I stared a second time at my newspaper in utter disbelief. The words hit me hard. "Poet, Michael Hartnett dies." I buried my face in my hands. One of my great joys in life was befriending Michael Hartnett. I simply could not believe the harrowing news.

There are moments in time when you stand on the brink of a new experience and understand that there is much more to learn. That was to be the case when I first met the inimitable Mr. Hartnett in Grogan's Pub on South William Street. Hartnett had passed a few pints behind his back to some Trinity College students and had established what seemed to be total control over them. In return, they seemed utterly devoted. The Limerick poet's legs looked like two strands of vermicelli. I had to look down to make sure his wobbly little feet were in fact touching terra firma. Yet with unerring aim, he hit the bar, holding the counter as he did so. "A brandy Sean, a brandy. Just a small one," he pleaded feebly. I was glad he got it.

At that time, little did I dream that his and my trails would cross through Dublin over the next six years and to this day I remain a great admirer of the solitary poet who would later read me out recipes for linguine with clam sauce, Basque white bean soup and duck with lime, with the same fascination he perused the works of St. Thomas Aquinas. Michael drifted through Dublin like a guideless ship with no anchor to keep in him in one place. I had never met someone like him before, certainly not head on. With such compassionate human material in front of me, there was never a dull moment.

---

*"There are three mythical figures in Ireland, Cú Chulainn, Fionn MacCumhaill and 'just the one'."*

---

My late friend Thérèse Cronin introduced us from afar. Michael tore up to us, bowed, kissed Thérèse's hand, then mine, graciously. 'Bhríd mo Chroí" He talked openly about his drunken imprisonment in Spain, how he was honoured with a literary prize in Sardinia, how he made mushroom pate almondine. He had John B. Keane's utter gift for language. The barman, Sean Kearney, noticing Hartnett's whizzy condition, thoughtfully ordered him a taxi. Hartnett grandly informed him that he was going home to cook 'boeuf en daube' for Angela, his partner of many years. "It's well for you," said Sean, "I'll be on the sausage and chips myself." With a flourish of his tweed cap, Hartnett reserved his full lung power for a recitation of 'Evelyn Hope,' by Browning. Then, with spellbinding stage charm, his tiny, tweedy frame disappeared in the back seat of the taxi, clutching his bag with a dead rabbit for tea and a bunch of artichokes. "There are three mythical figures in Ireland, you can quote me on this," he said as he leaned out of the taxi again, brushing his hair flat on his forehead, "Cú Chulainn, Fionn MacCumhaill and 'just the one'. I'll never forget that day, the impish glint in his eye, and the tears of laughter falling down my face.

There were to be prolonged drinking bouts ahead of me and great early morning discussions in Grogan's pub on literature, 'The Moosewood Cookbook,' and often one or two of the three seminal figures in his life; his Gaelic speaking grandmother, Bridget Halpin, the Irish poet and Sean-nós singer, Caitlín Maude, and the Kerry poet and philosopher, John Stephen Moriarty. Now that I think of it, I only ever encountered Michael in the morning time. He was an early riser, and I often had the feeling that by the time I met him, usually around eleven o'clock, his day was nearly over. A staunch admirer of his poetry and his exotic recipes, I always knew instinctively he would be fun

to interview. "I'm big in Finland," was one of his many comic refrains. I enjoyed his company so much. I put the interview off for years. I knew too much. When we finally agreed to an official interview, I realised that fun has a price. We met in the Leeson Lounge. The welcome was magnificent. "This is for you," he said, handing me a beautiful sunflower.

I had no idea that I would be letting myself into a three-day odyssey of drink, food, talk and craic. The barflies we met along the way did. "Four millionaires, a broken poet, and a journalist," said Michael tripping himself into a horizontal bow. "May I introduce Brighid McLaughlin from *The Sunday Independent*."

Safely slumped at the front of the bar, one of his cronies was riling Ireland's greatest living poet. "Where's the champagne Michael? This is a celebration." Hartnett produced his empty black lady's purse and burst into song.

"Look at me now, with my empty pockets, with my back to the wall, Mise Raifteirí an file, lán dóchais is grá. Look at me now, the poet with his arse to the wall and a purse with sweet fuck all." This was followed by raucous laughter. "Conor Cruise O'Brien told me not to grovel like a mole. So I won't."

I was mesmerised throughout, as he intended. Hartnett was also acting the innocent country simpleton, a part he loved playing, the Gaelic bard, the inscrutable satirist, was in rousing form. Like most geniuses, he wove a web of comic conspiracy into which I was drawn unawares. That day he insisted calling into the Spar shop on Baggot Street. A grand bow. Then the launderette. Another bow. Then the 'charcuterie'. Another bow, which resulted in a bottle of vodka on credit. "I need one more drink," said Michael, peering at the door of the Leeson Lounge as we passed by. "I'm not going in," I said defiantly. "But you're my credibility factor." Before I could utter a syllable, I was standing in front of the barman. The whole interview was an exhausting experience, which tired me out no end. Yet, I loved his company and he kept me perpetually amused. We finally made it to his home beside the Brigidine Convent on Dartmouth Road. "More Brighids," he sighed.

The basement flat where he then lived was a huge one – and stretched down a perspective of rooms to long French windows leading onto a lawn of shrubs. "Oh wild garlic," said Michael, "wonderful garlic, food from the Gods. And the birds...oh, the birds, God's little creatures." The room was pervaded by the sweet heavy scent of lilies. It was a tidy room where there was not the slightest sign its occupant ever did any work. Michael played Sibelius's violin concertos "to calm the nerves….if I get a writing block, I am in despair. As you well know, I drink too much. Drink causes despair." Family photographs were neatly framed on the sideboard. "That's my girlfriend, Angela," he said proudly. "I adore her." Then, with the sly twinkle of an adorable pet, he raised his glass, "To love. To life."

His favourite role as the awful rogue, the terrible liar had its own disarming charm, but it was his status as a 'real poet,' who was producing a considerable body of brilliant work in addition to his epicurean adventures which gained my fullest admiration.

His notorious abandonment of the English language in 1975, to which he had dedicated his life, remained so extraordinary that critics even friends, found it hard to explain, and so the subject was avoided. In 'A Farewell to English,' he called English "the perfect language to sell pigs in," and vowed to abandon it for "the language of my people".

It took him nearly ten years to change his mind and publish in English, 'Inchicore Haiku', was the starting point.

An Áosdána member and an American Ireland Fund Literary Award winner in 1990, Hartnett no longer had to ply his old trades, such as tea boy, "plunger" (dishwasher) or telephonist, as he once did.

"Michael has this sense of paganism, in the wildest sense," observed the late Dennis O'Driscoll. I agree whole-heartedly. A lot of Hartnett's poetry lambasts hypocrisies in the Catholic Church; even more of it displays a reverence for nature, for food and for the countryside. He was profoundly spiritual in the real sense of the word.

On the 27th January 1998, while visiting a friend, I bumped into Michael in the Foyer of St. Patrick's Hospital Dublin. He was "drying out" in the Laraco Unit and looked completely despondent, his sad compassionate eyes following the carpet. It was pitiful to see him in such a bad way. I could have cried. And I didn't need a crystal ball to see what was going to happen. His head was bent down and he was carrying a book on St. John of The Cross. Yet, the humour never failed. "The most brilliant people I know have been in institutions Brighid, I worry about the ones who haven't. There is no certification of sanity for them!"

In the canteen he talked about drink a lot. "I'm a binge drinker, a binge drinker," he said nodding his head sadly. "Poor Angela, I don't know how she puts up with me. I don't care what they say in here,

alcoholics can articulate the truth. Le vin la verite," he sighed. "I used to drink two bottles of brandy a day. Yesterday Professor Turley asked me if I was a secret drinker. "Jesus, there's nothing secret about it. Every dog in the street knows how much I drink."

"Did you see the portrait that Graham Knuttel did of me? Sylvester Stallone has it in Hollywood." He was chuffed about that.

In February I called up to the hospital to see him again. His room was suitably frugal. A bed, a suitcase, a simple painted cross stood on his table. Michael was reading Mistress Meg Dodd's Scottish cookbook. "I have to," he laughed. "The food here is awful. Did you ever hear of Bán bia?" he said. "During the famine, all the foods we ate were white and we were ahead of our time. We Irish ate yoghurt, garlic cheese and pork. So much for the yuppies. They don't realise that the grub they are digesting is as ancient as their ancestors."

Both avid cooks, we talked about Elizabeth David's books and Michael's recipe for ricotta pancakes. We found escape and comfort in cooking. You read the ingredients, measure, whisk, mix and create. All stress is forgotten. You simply beat and roll it out of you, the same way that you do in life. He handed me an apple; "it's called a Bismark apple," he said, looking at it as only a poet would.

For a small man, Michael was loved hugely. I will never forget him swaying out of the Westbury Hotel entrance, with his tweed cap stuck jauntily on the back of his head, lustily chanting Robert Service's 'Arctic Trails.'

At his funeral, which I couldn't bear to attend, Dr Tony Carroll, a dear friend compared burying Michael to "burying a child." He was wonderfully childlike and gentle. Nor shall I forget his sad frame one Halloween nursing a pumpkin faced candle in Grogan's. His was a persona for Technicolor memory. Right now I have one of his poems in front of me. This is an extract from 'Mo Ghrá Thú'.*

Nothing compares to Michael, his poetry or his cooking. I think of him often, particularly when I am cooking rabbit, one of his favourite dishes.

*'Mo Ghrá Thú' by Michael Hartnett from 'Collected Poems' (2001) by kind permission of the author's Estate and The Gallery Press, Loughcrew, Oldcastle, Co Meath.

'Mo Ghrá Thú'

"with me, so you call me man,

stay: winter is harsh to us,

my self is worth no money.

but with your self spread over me,

eggs under woodcock-wings,

the grass will not be meagre:

where we walk will be white

flowers."

# VEGETARIAN

# creamy CORN
# with CHEESE + POLENTA

*serves 2*

Biddy decided to visit me for a Bondi summer earlier this year, so we could work together and finish this book (any excuse for a holiday). We had the best time writing and researching (read: stuffing ourselves with Sydney's finest foods!). On the very last night, we treated ourselves to a meal at chef Peter Gilmore's restaurant, Bennelong, at The Sydney Opera House. The menu was incredible – I had an amazing polenta and corn dish. There was already a creamed corn recipe in this book, but we decided to update it and add polenta, to preserve the memory of that special night. This creation needs to be eaten right after it's made to catch the polenta at its smoothest, so be ready to serve immediately.

2 teaspoons ghee or butter

2 cobs corn, husks removed and kernels sliced

sea salt & cracked black pepper, to taste

2 tablespoons pine nuts

½ brown onion, finely chopped

2 cloves garlic, crushed

1 tablespoon dry white wine

⅓ cup (80ml) single (pouring) cream

⅓ cup (80ml) boiling water

## CREAMY POLENTA

1 litre vegetable or chicken stock

1 cup (250ml) milk

1 cup (170g) fine polenta (cornmeal)

¼ cup (60ml) cream

20g butter

½ cup (40g) parmesan

2 tablespoons crispy dried shallots, to serve

40g blue cheese, crumbled

sage leaves, to serve

Preheat oven to 180°C (350°F). Line a baking tray with non-stick baking paper.

Place half the ghee and the corn kernels on the prepared tray and season with salt and pepper. Roast for 5 minutes or until slightly soft.

Place the pine nuts on a baking tray and roast for 5 minutes or until golden.

Place the remaining ghee in a medium non-stick frying pan over medium heat. Add the onion and garlic and cook, stirring, for 5–10 minutes or until translucent. Add the wine and cook for 1 minute or until reduced. Add the cream and water, stir to combine and allow to thicken for 2–3 minutes. Transfer the mixture to a blender and add half the corn kernels. Blend until smooth. Pour into a bowl and stir through the remaining corn. Set aside and keep warm.

Place the stock and milk in a large saucepan over high heat. Bring to the boil and gradually add the polenta, whisking constantly. Cook for 2–3 minutes or until the polenta starts to thicken. Reduce the heat to low and simmer for 30 minutes or until smooth, stirring regularly. Add the cream, butter, parmesan, salt and pepper and stir until warmed through and combined.

Divide the polenta between serving bowls immediately and spoon over the corn sauce. Top with the pine nuts, crispy shallots, blue cheese and sage leaves to serve.

# MUSHROOM
## *à la crème* PIE

*serves* 4

I've been a pescetarian (a vegetarian who eats fish) for about 10 years now. On one of our first dates, my (now) fiancé invited me to his house for dinner – he knew the way to my heart. Delighted with my luck, I arrived only to find a room full of college boys and a chicken curry on the stove. While I was assured I could 'pick the chicken out' of my meal, it wasn't quite the romantic dinner I'd been dreaming of! Thankfully since then, he's been cooking amazing vegetarian food for me. A cooking course with Darina Allen in *Ballymaloe* gave him an incredible repertoire, and I feel very lucky to have him in our kitchen. This pie is a recipe from there that he's tweaked and it ticks all the right boxes. Creamy, with earthy flavours of onion, garlic and mushroom, it's pure winter heaven. The only down-side was that it took so long to make. But now that we have Trudi's easy-peasy pastry recipe (see *recipe*, page 174) we make it to our hearts' content.

*1 tablespoon butter*

*4 cloves garlic, sliced*

*1 onion, finely chopped*

*sea salt & cracked black pepper, to taste*

*1 tablespoon extra virgin olive oil*

*700g mixed mushrooms, roughly chopped*

*½ cup (125ml) single (pouring) cream*

*100g cream cheese, chopped*

*1 x quantity trudi's easy-peasy pastry (see recipe, page 174)*

*1 cup (120g) grated cheddar or gruyère*

*1 egg, lightly beaten, for brushing*

*thyme sprigs, to serve*

*finely grated parmesan, to serve*

Preheat oven to 180°C (350°F).

Melt the butter in a small saucepan over low heat. Add half the garlic and the onion, cover with a tight-fitting lid and cook for 5–10 minutes or until soft, stirring occasionally. Sprinkle with salt and pepper.

Place the oil in a large frying pan over high heat. Add the mushrooms, the remaining garlic, salt and pepper and cook, stirring, for 5–10 minutes or until soft. Reduce the heat to low and add the onion mixture to the mushroom mixture, stirring to combine. Add the cream and cream cheese and bring to a simmer. Cook for 15 minutes or until reduced. Allow to cool a little.

While the filling is simmering, divide the pastry in half and place one piece in a 28cm-round (4cm-deep) pie dish. Using your fingertips, press the pastry evenly into the base and sides of the dish, patching up any holes. Bake for 10 minutes. Roll out the remaining pastry on a lightly floured surface into a thin round to roughly fit the top of your pie dish.

Transfer the mushroom filling to the pastry case and sprinkle with the cheddar. Top with the pastry round, pressing the edges to seal and trimming to fit. Cut a cross in the centre of the pie and brush the top with the egg. Bake for 25–30 minutes or until golden brown. Serve topped with the thyme and parmesan.

*easy-peasy* LEEK +
*double* CHEESE QUICHE

*serves* 4

Ever since meeting Trudi and getting her pastry recipe (see *recipe*, page 174), I've been making quiche nearly every week! I just use whatever's in the fridge.

This combo is hands-down the best I've tried, so I wanted to share it. The leek has a beautiful caramelised flavour and the gruyère is mild and creamy in the fluffy eggs. Best of all, you can keep it in the fridge for up to a week, so it's a perfect snack. Make sure the tin you use has a removable base.

*1 x quantity trudi's easy-peasy pastry (see recipe, page 174)*

*2 leeks, trimmed and sliced*

*2 cups (240g) grated gruyère or cheddar*

*2 tablespoons chopped chives, plus extra to serve*

*4 eggs*

*¾ cup (180ml) cream*

*¾ cup (180ml) milk*

*1 teaspoon dijon mustard*

*1 teaspoon plain (all-purpose) flour*

*sea salt & cracked black pepper, to taste*

*2 tablespoons finely grated parmesan*

Preheat oven to 200°C (400°F). Place the pastry in a 28cm-round non-stick fluted loose-based quiche tin. Using your fingertips, press the pastry evenly into the base and sides of the tin, patching up any holes. Spread the leek, gruyère and chives evenly over the base.

Place the eggs, cream, milk, mustard, flour, salt and pepper in a medium bowl and whisk to combine. Pour into the quiche tin over the leek mixture.

Bake for 10 minutes on the middle shelf (so the heat can reach the base making it nice and crispy). Reduce the oven temperature to 180°C (350°F) and bake for a further 30 minutes. Allow to cool in the tin for 5 minutes.

Sprinkle with the parmesan and extra chives and slice to serve.

# SWEET POTATO *fritters* *with* CASHEW CREAM

*makes* 8

Fritters are something I discovered when I moved to Sydney. I lived with a girl from New Zealand and they were a staple in her diet. Every evening, she'd be making fritters from all sorts of vegetables. This sweet potato version is divine. They get nice and crispy on the edges but also have a kind of chewy texture that just melts in your mouth. I love them with fresh coriander and cashew cream, but they're also amazing with poached eggs for breakfast.

*2 cups (250g) grated sweet potato (kumara) (about 2 sweet potatoes)*

*2 tablespoons plain (all-purpose) flour*

*1 egg*

*1 tablespoon milk or almond milk*

*sea salt & cracked black pepper, to taste*

*1 tablespoon coconut oil*

*cashew cream with lemon zest (see recipe, page 182)*
*or plain greek-style (thick) yoghurt, to serve*

*coriander (cilantro) leaves, to serve*

Place the sweet potato, flour, egg, milk, salt and pepper in a large bowl and mix well to combine. Using clean hands, shape 1 tablespoon of the mixture into a ball and flatten into a patty. Repeat with the remaining mixture.

Heat a little of the oil in a medium non-stick frying pan over medium heat. Cook the patties, in batches, for 3–4 minutes each side or until golden, adding more oil as necessary. Remove from the pan and place on paper towel, keeping the fritters warm until ready to serve.

Divide between serving plates and top with the cashew cream and coriander.

# SWEET + CRISPY
# TEMPEH *poppers*

*serves 2*

More and more people in Ireland are making the decision to become vegetarian or cut down on meat. This doesn't mean they have to eat boring food! You'll believe me once you try these sweet, salty and crunchy bites of goodness, made from tempeh, which is similar to tofu, only firmer. Perfect for a snack or served on a bed of steamy rice with Asian greens for dinner.

¼ cup (60ml) soy sauce

2 tablespoons brown sugar

2–3 tablespoons coconut oil

1 x 300g packet tempeh, sliced into 5mm pieces

1 green onion (scallion), trimmed and thinly sliced

4 cloves garlic, thinly sliced

2 french shallots (eschalots), thinly sliced

1 medium red chilli, halved, seeded and sliced

2 kaffir lime leaves, torn

Place the soy sauce and sugar in a small saucepan over medium heat and cook, stirring, for 5 minutes or until thickened. Set aside.

Heat 2 tablespoons of the oil in a large non-stick frying pan or wok over high heat. When the oil is hot and bubbling, add half the tempeh and shallow-fry for 3 minutes each side or until golden brown and very crispy. Remove and set aside on paper towel. Repeat with the remaining tempeh, adding more oil if necessary.

Reduce the heat to medium and add the onion, garlic, shallot and chilli. Cook, stirring, for 1–2 minutes or until softened, adding more oil to the pan if necessary.

Return the fried tempeh to the pan. Add the soy mixture and lime leaves and toss gently to coat. Serve immediately as fingerfood or as a main meal with steamed rice and greens.

---

NOTE – The tempeh must be super golden and crispy when fried, so it keeps its crunch when the sauce is added.

---

VEGETARIAN

# BAKED TURNIP *with* GRUYÈRE + PRUNES

*serves* 4

People often ask me about turnips in Irish cooking. The Irish turnip is actually a swede, it's much bigger and has a different flavour and colour to other varieties of turnip, which tend to be small and white. In Ireland, a big dollop of orange mashed turnip with a melting knob of butter has forever been a beloved, sentimental side dish. This recipe is rich, creamy and unctuous. It can be served as an indulgent accompaniment to a meal, or as a vegetarian main course. This is comfort food at its best and despite the cream, cheese and butter, you can always console yourself with the knowledge that turnips are a good source of vitamin A, D and folic acid.

*2 cups (500ml) vegetable stock*

*1.2kg turnips, trimmed and peeled*

*sea salt & cracked white pepper, to taste*

*½ cup (120ml) double (thick) cream*

*1 teaspoon finely chopped thyme leaves, plus extra to serve*

*4 cloves garlic, sliced*

*1 pinch ground nutmeg*

*1¾ cups (220g) soft (ready-to-eat) pitted prunes*

*1½ cups (185g) finely grated gruyère*

Preheat oven to 150°C (300°F). Lightly grease a shallow 20cm x 30cm baking dish.

Place the stock in a large saucepan over medium heat and bring to the boil.

Cut the turnips into quarters, then cut them into 5mm-thick slices. Add to the stock with a little salt and pepper and cover with a tight-fitting lid. Cook for 10–15 minutes or until just soft but still intact and most of the liquid has been absorbed. Remove from the heat. Drain, reserving 1 cup (250ml) of the cooking liquid, and set aside.

Place the cream in a small saucepan over medium heat and add the thyme, garlic, nutmeg, salt, pepper and the reserved cooking liquid. Stir to combine, bring to the boil, then set aside to cool.

Arrange one-third of the turnip slices in a layer on the base of the prepared dish. Top with one-third of the prunes, cream mixture and gruyère. Repeat the layering 2 more times, finishing with the last of the gruyère.

Cover with aluminium foil and bake for 45 minutes or until soft enough to slice. Remove the foil and turn the oven grill (broiler) to high for the last 5 minutes of the cooking time or until the top is golden and melted. Sprinkle with the extra thyme leaves to serve.

# a trip to longford for
# BOXTY

*It was raining heavily when we hit the road for Longford and Leitrim, yet the mere thought of buttered golden boxty quickened our hearts...*

*Michael, rummaging in the clay, gathered the first four spuds from Kathleen's field.*

A 'grater' that had been made from a used biscuit tin which had holes punched through it with a nail.

"**B**oxty in the griddle, boxty in the pan; if you can't make boxty, you'll never get a man."

You rarely hear much about boxty these days, but in the countryside, especially Leitrim, Longford, Cavan and South Donegal it is still much loved. These golden, crispy, delicious little potato cakes, fried in butter, are truly addictive. Who knew there are so many different types of boxty: boxty loaf; boxty pancakes; boiled boxty; even fried boxty. It is a seasonal dish that comes into its own in September – why? Because that's when our Irish spuds are ready to be gathered in.

When Michael Masterson, my trusty rural 'private eye', informed me there was lady called Kathleen Conefry in Leitrim well known for her boxty making, I was not only intrigued, but begged him for a meeting.

The sky was covered in a fine cloud when Kady and I arrived in Longford two weeks later, and a great fuss developed when Kathleen saw the camera.

"Oh, no–o–o, I don't want photographs taken of me," she cried hiding behind a tea towel.

"If the Italians like spaghetti, we have the same addiction to boxty," she laughs, bright eyed and ruddy. "Boxty is a big job," warns Kathleen. "It often takes me three hours to make it – it's a comfort food. Actually, my traditional recipes were called 'Comeragh cakes'."

Outside in her field, Kady and I help Kathleen gather 20 or so potatoes. "I use Roosters or Kerr Pinks, three-quarters of them have to be grated raw." She goes to the basin and washes her hands. Now, all her attention is taken up with grating the potatoes.

"When someone calls in to visit, you just can't stop grating. You have to keep on working at it otherwise the potato will discolour. You have to keep quiet – God help anyone who might ask a question."

In the pleasure of watching her repeat a process that is likely hundreds of years old in Ireland, I found myself utterly immersed in her rhythm and quiet.

"It's all about the raw potatoes more than the boiled," she says gently. "You need a mix of cold mashed potato and grated raw potato. 3 parts raw and 1 part mash. A fistful of flour (half a cup). A big pinch of salt. There's nothing added except time. When you are done grating your raw potatoes, you fill a cotton bag or clean pillowcase with them and then squeeze the liquid starch out of the bag. Be careful not to over-wring it.

"You want it damp, but not too dry, this gives more of a grain to the boxty. Then grease the pan with butter. In South Longford, boxty was known as 'rasp' boxty because of the sound it made hitting the butter in the pan."

Suddenly, Kathleen remembered to show me one of her favourite tools – a rather primitive looking utensil, a 'grater' that had been made from a used biscuit tin which had holes punched through it with a nail. I found the object fascinating and ingenious.

"When I make boxty, I text my son Tommy in Dublin with just one word – boxty. He'd nearly leave Coppers (a famous nightclub in Dublin) to get home for it."

THE H

UMBLE POTATO

# kathleen's *TRADITIONAL* BOXTY *loaf*

*makes* 1 *loaf*

Boxty is one of the forgotten glories of Irish gastronomy. But thankfully, those golden buttery pancakes, solid with grated and mashed potato are kept alive by communities in Cavan, Leitrim, Longford and south Donegal. In Dublin, there is a bit of a revival going on at the moment, with butchers now stocking and slicing boxty cake for regulars who cannot get enough of it. Boxty is a really practical dish that costs almost nothing to make. There are many variations to the recipes – you can make boxty loaf in a tin and have it sliced, then fried, and there are the famous boxty pancakes, which are often cut into triangles, My favourite boxty are the little cakes in bubbling butter on the pan. I cannot help but get a feeling of warmth and gratitude as I wait for them to crisp. As each piece of fried boxty is opened, you are certain to find gorgeous grated potato inside. A sprinkling of salt and pepper, and all is well in the world.

*4kg floury potatoes, peeled (rooster, kerr's pink or coliban varieties work best)*

*½ cup (75g) plain (all-purpose) flour*

*1 teaspoon sea salt flakes, plus extra to serve*

*2 tablespoons butter*

Preheat oven to 150°C (300°F). Lightly grease a 10cm x 20cm loaf tin.

Roughly chop 1.5kg of the potatoes and place them in a large saucepan. Cover with cold water and place over medium heat. Bring to the boil and simmer for 15 minutes or until tender. Drain well and return to the pan. Mash until smooth.

While the potatoes are boiling, coarsely grate the remaining 2.5kg potatoes and place them in a large sieve lined with muslin. Press to remove the liquid (you could also squeeze them dry in a large clean tea towel). Add the drained potato to the mashed potato and mix to combine. Add the flour, salt and butter and mix to combine.

Place the mixture into the prepared tin and bake for 1 hour 30 minutes or until cooked through and golden.

Turn out of the tin and slice as you would a loaf of bread. Serve immediately with a sprinkling of salt, or pan-fry slices in a little butter until golden and crispy.

*biddy's simple*
# GNOCCHI

*serves 4*

Gnocchi is truly divine when it's pillowy and soft – it just melts in your mouth. There are a few tricks to getting this delicious consistency, and after years of cooking this recipe, I've listed them below. It's worth noting that in Italy there are many different shaped gnocchis. You can press them gently with a fork to make ridges (great for absorbing sauce) or leave them as rustic little rounds.

*coarse rock salt, for roasting*

*4–5 medium floury potatoes (800g) (coliban or king edward varieties work best)*

*⅔ cup (100g) 00 flour, plus extra for dusting*

*½ cup (40g) finely grated parmesan*

*¼ teaspoon ground white pepper*

*1 teaspoon sea salt flakes*

*2 large eggs, at room temperature*

Preheat oven to 200°C (400°F). Line a baking tray with rock salt. Pierce each potato (peel on) all over with a skewer, then place on the tray. Roast for 30 minutes or until cooked through.

Carefully halve the hot potatoes and allow to cool for 10 minutes. Scoop the potato out of the skins and using a potato ricer, rice the potatoes, one half at a time, until fine.

Weigh the riced potatoes and adjust the amount of flour accordingly, to a ratio of 5:1 (i.e. for 500g riced potato you'll need 100g flour). Spread the potato onto a clean, dry surface and sift three-quarters of the flour (from a height) over the top. Add the parmesan, pepper and salt.

Separate 1 of the eggs and place the yolk in a small bowl (reserving the white for a different use). Add the remaining egg to the bowl and lightly whisk to combine. Add half the egg mixture to the potato mixture and gently bring together, using a fork. If necessary, add the remaining egg and flour, and gently press to form a light, malleable dough (don't knead or overwork it). Transfer the dough to a clean, floured surface and cut it into quarters. Using floured hands, roll the pieces into logs, then slice them diagonally into 2cm pillows.

Press gently with a fork to shape, if you like. Arrange the gnocchi on a tray and cover with a clean tea towel. Chill until ready to cook.

To cook the gnocchi, bring a large shallow saucepan of water to a simmer over medium heat. Add the gnocchi and cook for 3 minutes or until risen to the surface. Remove with a slotted spoon and serve with a pasta sauce (like our walnut sauce with ginger cream, *see recipe*, page 183) or some sage and garlic butter.

———————

NOTES – 00 flour is a superfine flour, traditionally used for baking and pizza dough. Find it in the baking aisle of supermarkets or at Italian grocers.

Roasting the pierced potatoes on a salt bed helps to draw out any moisture (the enemy of gnocchi). A light touch makes the best gnocchi. Press it with gentle hands and avoid kneading (tempting as it is). Floury potatoes like King Edward or Coliban make for lovely, fluffy pillows.

By weighing the riced potatoes, you'll get a more accurate feel for how much flour to use. It also means you can tailor this recipe to your desired quantity, should you need to.

Potato ricers are like a large garlic press and leave no lumps in your mash. They can be found in any kitchen shop. In Dublin, try *Kitchen Compliments* or *Anvil* in Bray.

*baby potato* SCONES
*with* SCALLIONS + HERBS

*makes* 14

These delicious little savoury scones are great as an accompaniment for soup, or as an entree, topped with egg salad and chives or smoked salmon. If you like your scones higher, stack two together with cream cheese or butter in between.

*1½ cups (225g) self-raising (self-rising) flour, plus extra for dusting*

*½ teaspoon baking powder*

*sea salt & cracked white pepper, to taste*

*65g butter, chopped, at room temperature*

*3 green onions (scallions), trimmed and finely chopped*

*1 tablespoon dried oregano or thyme leaves*

*⅔ cup (150g) mashed potato (about 1 medium potato)*

*⅓ cup (40g) grated vintage cheddar*

*⅓ cup (80ml) buttermilk*

*1 egg, lightly beaten with a little water*

*dried chives, to serve*

Preheat oven to 200°C (400°F). Lightly grease a 20cm x 30cm slice tin.

Sift the flour, baking powder, salt and pepper into a large bowl from a height (to aerate). Add the butter and, using your fingertips, rub into the flour until the mixture resembles breadcrumbs. Add the onion and oregano and mix until just combined. Add the potato, cheddar and enough of the buttermilk until a soft (not sticky) dough comes together.

Turn out the dough onto a lightly floured surface. Gently roll or press the dough out into a 4cm-thick round. Using a 5cm round cutter dipped in flour, cut as many scones as you can from the dough, re-rolling any scraps. Place them so they fit snugly in the prepared tin (they'll help each other rise)

Brush the scones with the egg and bake for 20 minutes or until golden brown on top. Serve warm with sliced cheddar, or top with your favourite savoury spread. Garnish with chives.

# smoky JOE

*serves 4*

If you asked me to name my favourite supper dish it would have to be Smoky Joe.
I first tasted it in the Trocadero, Dublin, a theatre restaurant which has attracted
stars of the stage and screen for nearly sixty years. This traditional dish is robust
and earthy, with an amazing combination of flavours (think flaky cooked smoked
salmon, floury potatoes, soft buttery onions, dill and capers). Slicing the potatoes
can take a little time but it's really worth it. Bake and tuck in on a winter's evening
or serve it cold in summer for lunch with a fresh crunchy salad.

*1.6kg floury potatoes (about 8 potatoes),*
*peeled (coliban or king edward varieties work best)*

*1 tablespoon butter, plus extra for greasing*

*1 large red onion, sliced into thin rounds*

*4 cloves garlic, finely chopped*

*½ cup (125ml) dry white wine*

*1¼ cups (310ml) vegetable stock, heated*

*juice and finely grated rind of 1 lemon*

*1 tablespoon chopped dill, plus extra to serve*

*300g sliced smoked salmon*

*1 tablespoon capers, drained*

*sea salt & cracked white pepper, to taste*

*1⅔ cups (410ml) single (pouring) cream*

*1¼ cups (100g) finely grated parmesan*

Place the potatoes in a large saucepan of salted boiling water over high heat and cook for 15 minutes
or until soft on the outside but still firm inside (you can test them with a sharp knife). Drain and allow to cool.

Melt the butter in a medium frying pan over medium heat. Add the onion and garlic and cook, stirring,
for 5 minutes or until translucent. Add the wine, stock, lemon juice, rind and dill, stir to combine and bring
to a simmer. Cook for a further 2–3 minutes or until slightly reduced.

Preheat oven to 200°C (400°F). Lightly grease a medium baking dish. Slice the cooled potatoes into
thin rounds. Line the base of the dish with a layer of potato. Top with one-third of the smoked salmon
and one-third of the onion mixture. Sprinkle with one-third of the capers and some salt and pepper.
Repeat to make 2 more even layers. Pour the cream over the top layer and sprinkle with the parmesan.
Bake for 30 minutes or until cooked through and golden brown. Sprinkle with the extra dill to serve.

# *from* DUBLIN'S FAIR CITY

*Philip as a child in his home in Ballyfermot, Dublin (above); with President Clinton (left); at a wedding in Dublin just before moving to Sydney, mullet still intact (right).*

P hilip Cronin is the Chairman of the Australian Information Industry Association and the former General Manager of Intel in Australia and New Zealand.

## CODDLE

*The name 'coddle' comes from the verb 'coddle', meaning to cook food in water below boiling.*

Coddle, originally created to use up leftovers, is a very old, much loved Dublin dish. This dish is intrinsically an economical comfort food that nourishes and protects from the cold. However, you either love it or you hate it. Some people dread the sight of a pale greasy white sausage, swimming above the watery broth. Being a pescitarean myself, you can imagine how I feel about it. Philip loves it, however, and this is his story.

We meet in the *Flour and Stone* Cafe in Darlinghurst, Sydney, a small cosy bustling coffee shop where they serve excellent beverages and dreamy tarts and cakes. I find Philip ordering an Earl Grey tea from the waitress. "I've already had two coffees," he says, one eye on the large fluffy meringues behind the counter. "I like the look of them," he says wistfully but resists because he is in training. "I am trekking to Papua, New Guinea, through rugged mountainous country, rainforests, jungles, the lot. I hate always being pegged as the 'IT' guy."

Philip's is the classic story of a working-class guy from the tough suburbs of Ballyfermot (Dublin), making it good in Australia. In fact, he has made it very good indeed. Philip is the Chairman of the Australian Information Industry Association, former General Manager of Intel for Australia and New Zealand and recently appointed President of the Australian Lansdowne Club. In addition to being super career-orientated and highly successful in the IT industry, like every good Irishman, Philip loves his grub, so we make a delicious shortcut to my favourite subject – food.

"The dish I really want to talk about is Dublin Coddle," says Philip with a hearty laugh. "It's a real Cronin tradition in Ballyfermot. It was usually served on Thursday, the reason being that most Dublin families were Catholics and didn't eat meat on a Friday." Coddle was a really inexpensive dish to make – sausages were cheap and bits of leftover bacon were added to it. "It needed to be cheap... there were 13 of us living in a tiny three-bedroom council house in Ballyfermot.

"In those days, people gathered up leftovers before the meat went off. Refrigeration wasn't an option.

My mother would start preparing it on Thursday morning. It was very simple to make, some fatty rashers (bacon), a couple of vegetables, potatoes (not that many), parsley. If you think of it now, this was very early slow-cooking at its best. When you came home from school, you would get a good, warm, hearty smell of coddle throughout the house and you'd be ladling it out. Sometimes I would burn the mouth off myself I was so hungry.

"To this day, a big bowl of soup is a really personal thing to me. The smell alone draws you in and makes me hungry just thinking about it.

"You could spend a good half an hour eating coddle. A lot of the taste is driven by the stock. You'd mop up the juices with a big slice of buttered soft white *Johnson, Mooney and O'Brien* sliced pan – another real Dublin institution. Heaven.

"By lunchtime on Thursday, it would nearly all be gone. There was never any second helpings. My Dad was in the army so I think the big bowls we used came from there.

"I remember the chunky potatoes that would still be whole, the sausage skins peeled back a little. When you taste it, despite its frugality (the fat has been boiled out of it), it's a really flavoursome, healthy winter dish."

Producing a snapshot of himself, taken in his twenties, with a hilarious mullet haircut, Philip tells me about his love for Australia.

"My older brother was living here at the time. After listening to him on the phone, I was all fired up about coming to Australia. It was November, the weather was lovely, both light and warmth at 7.30 in the morning. One day, we went to Bondi. I was speechless when I saw the beach. Just as we were about to step into the water for a swim, two drop dead gorgeous girls walked by and we looked at each other. That was it. From that moment I knew I was staying. From a mullet to Newtown! I had the mullet whacked off. I was 26 at the time. I felt like I was at a party every weekend.

"In my case, as far as my work is concerned, growing up in a working class area of Dublin was hugely important. My parents were very strong on education. They gave you a confidence and a brain that was ticking over. It gives you a tough edge. I never found it detrimental being Irish in Australia. It has worked for me in business and politics. Being Irish here, there's an ease of conversation that flows. Then it's down to business."

SOUP

# cold POTATO and APPLE *vichyssoise*

*serves 4*

This chilled, silky apple and potato soup is a little different to the infamous original vichyssoise. The potato and leek classic was arguably created in 1917, when Chef Lois Diat, of the Ritz Carlton, New York, was reminiscing about his French childhood – eating the soup his mother made, but first cooling it with milk. The apple in this variation adds a sweet but tart flavour. The soup can be served as a starter in tiny glasses or soup bowls when entertaining (handy for a busy host) or warm, too, if you prefer – just ensure it's not too hot when you add the cream.

*2 tablespoons butter*

*2 leeks, white part only, sliced into rounds*

*½ stalk celery, finely chopped*

*½ brown onion, finely chopped*

*1¾ cups (435ml) water*

*2½ medium floury potatoes, peeled and grated (russet or yukon gold varieties work best)*

*sea salt & cracked black pepper, to taste*

*1 fresh or dried bay leaf*

*1 pinch dried thyme leaves*

*2½ cups (625ml) vegetable stock*

*3 small golden delicious apples or 2 medium bramley apples (300g), peeled and chopped*

*2 teaspoons caster (superfine) sugar*

*1 teaspoon lemon juice*

*1¼ cups (310ml) double (thick) cream*

## CANDIED APPLE SLICES

*makes 10*

*butter, for greasing*

*1 medium granny smith apple, thinly sliced*

*1 tablespoon caster (superfine) sugar*

Melt the butter in a large non-stick frying pan over low heat. Add the leek, celery and onion and cook for 10 minutes. Add ½ cup (125ml) of the water, the potato, salt, pepper, bay and thyme. Stir well, cover with a tight-fitting lid and cook for 10 minutes. Increase the heat to high and add the stock. Bring to the boil, reduce the heat to low and simmer, partially covered, for 30 minutes. Allow to cool.

While the potato is simmering, place the apple in a medium saucepan over high heat. Add the remaining 1¼ cups (310ml) water, the sugar and lemon juice. Bring to the boil and simmer until soft. Allow to cool.

Place the potato mixture in a blender or food processor and add three-quarters of the apple mixture. Blend until smooth. Add the cream, stir to combine and refrigerate for 2–3 hours or overnight until chilled.

Divide the soup between serving bowls and top with the remaining stewed apple.

Decorate with candied apple slices, if you like. To do this, preheat oven to 200°C (400°F). Lightly grease a baking tray with butter. Arrange the apple on the tray and sprinkle with the sugar. Bake for 10 minutes or until golden and the sugar has dissolved. Allow to set on the trays.

# kady's MUSHROOM + CHESTNUT SOUP

*serves* 2–3

When I was young, I used to go mushroom picking, down by the banks of the Shannon, with my grandmother who knew all about them (and which ones not to pick, of course!). I loved it – running around with my brothers and sisters, seeing who could find the most. Then we'd head back to her house and make mushroom soup. It was so comforting, and I think where I inherited my love of mushrooms. There's something that connects you to produce when you're lucky enough to pick it yourself – let alone in such special company. This soup is very warming and satisfying – a perfect lunch for a winter's day.

*2 teaspoons ghee or butter*

*2 garlic cloves, finely chopped*

*1 medium brown onion, finely chopped*

*400g mixed mushrooms, sliced*

*1 tablespoon plain (all-purpose) flour*

*2½ cups (625ml) vegetable stock*

*2½ cups (625ml) milk*

*200g tinned chestnuts, finely chopped*

*sea salt & cracked black pepper, to taste*

*chopped tarragon leaves, to serve*

Heat half the ghee in a medium saucepan over low heat. Add the garlic and onion and cover with a tight-fitting lid. Cook, stirring occasionally for 10–15 minutes or until translucent and soft.

Heat the remaining ghee in a medium non-stick frying pan over high heat. Add the mushrooms and sauté for 10 minutes or until the mushrooms are soft and have darkened in colour. Transfer the mushrooms to the pan with the onion and garlic. Add the flour and cook, stirring, for 3–4 minutes or until well combined and bubbling.

While the mushrooms are cooking, place the stock and milk in a large saucepan over high heat and bring to the boil.

Gradually add the stock mixture to the mushroom mixture, stirring until combined and simmering. Add the chestnuts, salt and pepper and stir to combine.

Ladle into bowls and sprinkle with the tarragon to serve.

---

NOTE – I love to garnish this soup with marinated mushrooms, see *recipe* page 156.

---

# SWEET + SOUR
## *vegetable* SOUP

*serves 6*

I first discovered this unusual soup years ago in the classic
Moosewood Cookbook, by Mollie Katzen. It's a recipe that exudes confidence,
with its strong combination of spice and sweetness. I never knew you could use
apple juice blended with vegetable stock as a base for a soup until then.
Though I will say, it MUST be good-quality cloudy apple juice (cheap sweetened
juice will taste awful – I know from experience!). If you have only a basic juice
in your supermarket, consider juicing your own apples or buy some freshly
pressed and add water to make up the full 1 litre required.

*2 tablespoons butter*

*2 tablespoons extra virgin olive oil*

*1 medium brown onion, finely chopped*

*6 cloves garlic, finely chopped*

*1 teaspoon finely chopped ginger*

*1 tablespoon mild curry powder*

*2 teaspoons ground turmeric*

*500g carrots, peeled and chopped into rounds*

*450g parsnips, peeled and chopped into rounds*

*2 cups (500ml) vegetable stock*

*1 litre good-quality unsweetened cloudy apple juice*

*sea salt & cracked black pepper, to taste*

*400g potatoes (about 2 medium potatoes),
peeled and chopped into 2cm pieces*

*finely grated rind of ½ an orange*

*coriander (cilantro) leaves, to serve*

*single (pouring) cream, to serve*

Place the butter and oil in a large heavy-based saucepan over medium heat.
Add the onion, garlic and ginger and cook, stirring, for 5–10 minutes or until soft.
Add the curry powder and turmeric and cook, stirring, for 2–3 minutes or until fragrant.

Add the carrot, parsnip, stock, apple juice, salt and pepper and stir to combine.
Bring to the boil and allow to simmer for 20 minutes. Add the potato and cook for
a further 6–8 minutes or until the vegetables are just tender.

Divide between serving bowls and top with the orange rind, coriander
and a little cream to serve.

# *vietnamese* SOUR SOUP *with* SNAPPER

*serves 2*

Nothing says Irish cuisine quite like Vietnamese sour fish soup! Jokes aside, this dish was discovered on my travels around Vietnam and I've included it as a nod to all the beautiful Irish people I ate it with over there. We really know how to get around, us Irish! I love that more and more, we're bringing home new food influences from our travels abroad. This soup is packed full of flavour. Sour notes from the tamarind, pineapple to sweeten it – there are new notes discovered in every spoonful.

*2 tablespoons tamarind paste*

*1 litre boiling water*

*1 tablespoon extra virgin olive oil*

*2 cloves garlic, finely chopped*

*1 french shallot (eschalot), finely chopped*

*1 stalk lemongrass, white part only, crushed, peeled and finely chopped*

*1 small red chilli, seeded and finely chopped*

*2 skinless snapper fillets (550g), chopped into large pieces*

*1 stalk celery, trimmed and chopped*

*2 tomatoes, roughly chopped*

*1 cup (130g) chopped fresh pineapple*

*1 cup (80g) bean sprouts*

*1 tablespoon fish sauce*

*coriander (cilantro) leaves, to serve*

Place the tamarind and 1 cup (250ml) of the water in a medium jug. Mix to combine and set aside.

Heat the oil in a large heavy-based saucepan over medium heat. Add the garlic, shallot, lemongrass and chilli and cook, stirring, for 5 minutes or until fragrant. Add the tamarind mixture, stir to combine and bring to a simmer. Add the fish and celery and top with the remaining 3 cups (750ml) water. Return to the boil and allow to simmer for 5 minutes. Add the tomatoes and pineapple, stir to combine and cook for a further 5 minutes or until the fish is cooked through. Add the bean sprouts and fish sauce and stir to combine.

Divide the soup between serving bowls and top with plenty of coriander to serve.

NOTE – This soup is best enjoyed right away. It does not keep very well and should not be re-heated.

DES + SALADS

# full-o-beans SALAD

*serves 4*

This vibrant, crunchy fresh salad makes you feel alive. It's a beautifully nourishing bowl, with a lovely soft sweet twist of fig and velvety goat's cheese. Enjoy as it is, or pair it with crispy-skinned fish.

*50g macadamia nuts*

*200g green beans, trimmed and halved*

*200g snow peas (mange tout), trimmed*

*1 cup (25g) mixed salad leaves, washed and dried*

*150g dried figs, sliced*

*120g goat's cheese, crumbled*

*⅓ cup (80ml) sweetie sharpy salad dressing (see recipe, page 186)*

Preheat oven to 180°C (350°F). Place the nuts on a baking tray and roast for 5 minutes or until slightly golden and toasted. Allow to cool then roughly chop.

Place the beans and peas in a saucepan of salted boiling water and allow to stand for 5 minutes. Drain and rinse under cold running water to halt the cooking process. Allow to dry (you can use a salad spinner or clean tea towel if you like).

Place the salad leaves on a large platter and top with the beans, peas, figs and cheese. Drizzle with the dressing and sprinkle with the nuts to serve.

# the BIG ROAST salad

*serves 2*

There's something about roasted butternut squash that reminds me of autumn – all cosy and bright like the leaves, with that same comforting feeling. This salad captures its flavour and warmth. It's the perfect lunch for a cool day.

*1 tablespoon coconut oil*

*¼ butternut pumpkin (squash) (800g), peeled, seeded and cubed*

*1 red onion, thinly sliced*

*sea salt & cracked black pepper, to taste*

*2 cups (50g) baby rocket leaves*

*30g goat's cheese*

*1 tablespoon dried thyme leaves*

*1 teaspoon dried garlic granules*

*1 tablespoon dried cranberries*

*1 tablespoon slivered almonds*

**DELISH APPLE DRESSING**

*2 tablespoons extra virgin olive oil*

*1 teaspoon wholegrain mustard*

*1 tablespoon raw honey*

*1 tablespoon apple cider vinegar*

Preheat oven to 180°C (350°F). Place the coconut oil on a baking tray and heat in the oven for 3–5 minutes or until melted. Remove the tray from the oven and add the pumpkin and onion. Sprinkle with salt and pepper and toss to combine. Roast for 20–30 minutes or until soft.

To make the dressing, place the ingredients in a small bowl and whisk to combine.

Transfer the pumpkin and onion to a large salad bowl and add the rocket, cheese, dried thyme and garlic and the cranberries and almonds. Drizzle with the dressing and toss to combine.

# HALOU-MI *salad*

*serves* 2

What did the cheese say when it looked in the mirror? HELLO ME!
Sorry, I do love a good 'cheesy' joke. The haloumi in this recipe has just the
right amount of salt to offset the sweet succulent peach. Surprisingly filling
(for a salad, that is) you'll be very satisfied with this, for lunch or dinner.

### DELISH APPLE DRESSING

*2 tablespoons extra virgin olive oil*

*1 teaspoon wholegrain mustard*

*1 tablespoon raw honey*

*1 tablespoon apple cider vinegar*

*1 teaspoon ghee or butter*

*225g haloumi, sliced into 1cm-thick strips*

*3 cups (75g) baby rocket leaves*

*1 peach, pitted and sliced*

*1 avocado, seeded and sliced*

*½ red onion, thinly sliced (optional)*

*1 teaspoon store-bought dukkah, for sprinkling*

*½ lemon, cut into wedges*

To make the dressing, place the ingredients in a small bowl
and whisk to combine. Set aside.

Heat a large frying pan over medium heat. Add the ghee and then
the haloumi and cook for 3–4 minutes each side or until golden.

Arrange the rocket leaves, peach, avocado and onion on a serving
platter and top with the haloumi. Drizzle with the dressing and sprinkle
with the dukkah. Serve with a wedge of lemon for the haloumi.

# TAH*ini* BROCCOL*ini*

*serves* 2

I may be on my own here, but sometimes I just crave a big bowl of broccoli. I could eat a whole bunch, steamed with nothing but salt. I know not everyone shares this passion, so I've created a satiating salad with a creamy, earthy tahini sauce. Perfect with some barbecued fish or meat (if you need a little something else).

*1 bunch broccolini (175g)*

*2 tablespoons pistachios, roughly chopped*

**TAHINI DRESSING**

*½ small clove garlic*

*¼ cup (70g) hulled tahini*

*1 tablespoon lemon juice*

*¼ cup (60ml) hot water*

*sea salt & cracked black pepper, to taste*

Place the broccolini in a steamer set over a saucepan of simmering water and steam for 3–5 minutes or until tender.

To make the tahini dressing, crush the garlic into a small bowl and add the tahini, lemon juice, water, salt and pepper. Whisk to combine.

Place the broccolini onto a serving platter and drizzle with the dressing. Sprinkle with the pistachios to serve.

# *irish field* MUSHROOMS
# *with* DILLISK + CHESTNUTS

*serves* 4

I've been roasting field mushrooms on a griddle over the turf fire for years. On a winter's day in the cottage, the sound of rain typewriting on the roof, there's nothing as satisfying. I created this recipe one Halloween when I had a glut of chestnuts and a grand big bag of dillisk (Irish seaweed) from Urrismanagh, Donegal. The combination of seaweed and chestnut crumb is phenomenal. I'm inclined to indulge in these earthy delights with ill-conceived satisfaction.

170g tinned chestnuts, drained, dried and chopped
(you can also use fresh or vacuum-packed chestnuts)

½ cup finely chopped dried dillisk (dulse)

250g field mushrooms (about 4 large mushrooms)

25g butter

cracked white pepper, to taste

½ teaspoon dried oregano

Preheat oven to 180°C (350°F). Lightly grease 2 baking trays.

Spread the chestnut and dillisk on 1 of the prepared trays and bake for 5 minutes or until dry.

Brush the mushrooms with a dry cloth to remove any dirt and remove the skin if necessary. Remove the stalks. Place the mushrooms, top-side down, on the second prepared tray. Place a knob of butter in the centre of each mushroom, then drop 1 heaped tablespoon of the chestnut and dillisk crumb on top. Sprinkle with the pepper and oregano. Roast for 10 minutes or until cooked through.

# SHIITAKE HAPPENS

*makes 6 cups*

Our friend, mycologist Bill O'Dea at Mushroomstuff subjected us to a taste of his marinated shiitake mushrooms last year and since then we are hooked! Inspired by a dish at Momofuku Noodle Bar in New York, his shiitake mushrooms are really tasty but they are also high in fibre, vitamin D, selenium and other essential nutrients. They're used extensively in Chinese medicine.

For more information on the health benefits of mushrooms go to *mushroomstuff.com*

*2 cups (500ml) water*

*1 cup (250ml) good-quality soy sauce*

*1 cup (250ml) good-quality red wine vinegar*

*1 cup (220g) caster (superfine) sugar*

*1 x 4cm piece ginger, sliced*

*4 cups (120g) dried shiitake mushrooms, stems removed*

Place the water, soy, vinegar, sugar and ginger in a medium saucepan over medium heat. Bring to the boil, stirring to dissolve the sugar. Add the mushrooms and weigh them down with a small heatproof plate or lid to stop them floating. Reduce the heat to low and simmer gently for 30 minutes.

Allow to cool completely in the saucepan, before transferring into sterilised jars, ensuring the mushrooms in each jar are submerged in the marinade. Seal and keep refrigerated for up to 6 months (they'll become more flavourful with age).

———

NOTE – from Bill O'Dea: "The better quality the red wine vinegar, the better quality the mushrooms."

EADS + BAKING

# GARLIC + ROSEMARY *focaccia*

*makes* 1 *large loaf*

The smells wafting from your kitchen as you make this bread are incredible.
A heads up that it does take a little time, however, it's easy to do – perfect
for a weekend when you're at home. It's worth it for this fine-textured, fluffy
bread with a golden garlic and rosemary crust. Pair it with soups, salads or
deli-style cheesy toasted sandwiches (stuffed with fresh tomato or tangy
artichokes). It keeps really well for a few days, too.

*1kg 00 flour, plus extra for dusting*

*1 teaspoon dried yeast*

*2¾ cups (690ml) tepid water*

*1½ teaspoons sea salt flakes, plus extra for sprinkling*

*½ cup (125ml) extra virgin olive oil, plus extra for greasing*

*10 cloves garlic, thinly sliced*

*6 sprigs rosemary, leaves picked*

Sift the flour and yeast into a large bowl. Add the water and stir until
the mixture comes together, adding a little extra if necessary. Cover with
a warm damp tea-towel and allow to stand for 30 minutes.

Add the salt and turn the mixture out onto a floured surface. Knead for
5 minutes or until smooth. Lightly grease a clean, dry bowl with the extra oil
and add the dough. Cover with the tea-towel and set aside for 1 hour.

Lightly grease a 30cm x 40cm baking tray or slice tin with the extra oil. Turn
out the dough again onto a floured surface. Roll out and shape it to roughly
fit your prepared tray, then place it in, pressing gently so it reaches the edges.
Gently press your fingertips all over the dough to create a dimpled effect.
Allow to stand for 1 hour or cover and refrigerate overnight.

Preheat oven to 200°C (400°F). Place the oil, garlic and rosemary in a
bowl and mix to combine. Pour the mixture over the dough and brush
to cover evenly. Bake for 20 minutes or until golden brown and cooked
through. Allow to cool in the tin for 10 minutes, then turn out, sprinkle
with extra salt and slice to serve.

*gluten-free*

# MEDITERRANEAN *bread*

*makes* **1** *small loaf*

I make a loaf of this bread whenever I'm taking a break from gluten, dairy and sugar in my diet (I'll sometimes give my body a rest from these tricky-to-digest but delicious ingredients). I'm a complete bread obsessive, so I had to find something good to substitute. It has great flavour (my fiancé actually prefers it to regular wheat bread, and that's saying something!), plus you can make it all in one bowl and there's no proving of the dough required – easy. It keeps really well and is super-tasty when toasted. Hint: don't be tempted to chop the onion – it needs to be grated for the dough to hold.

*1½ cups (180g) almond meal (ground almonds)*

*½ cup (30g) psyllium husks*

*2 tablespoons nutritional yeast*

*1½ teaspoons baking powder*

*1 large brown onion, finely grated*

*2 cloves garlic, crushed*

*2 tablespoons semi-dried tomatoes, drained and chopped*

*4 green (sicilian) olives, pitted and sliced*

*½ teaspoon sea salt flakes*

*cracked black pepper*

*2 eggs*

*1 teaspoon ground turmeric*

*1 tablespoon chopped rosemary leaves (optional)*

*3 tablespoons mixed seeds; try flax, poppy and pumpkin seeds (pepitas)*

Preheat oven to 180°C (350°F). Line a 10cm x 20cm loaf tin with non-stick baking paper.

Place all the ingredients except the mixed seeds in a large bowl and mix until really well combined. Add 2 tablespoons of mixed seeds and stir. Pour into the prepared tin and spread evenly. Sprinkle the remaining tablespoon of seeds over the top. Bake for 35 minutes or until golden and cooked when tested with a skewer.

Allow to cool slightly in the tin, before lifting out and slicing to serve.

---

NOTE - You'll find most of these ingredients in the health-food aisle of the supermarket or from health food shops. I also love *iherb.com*.

# *treacle* BREAD

*makes* 1 *large loaf*

Treacle bread has a long history in Ireland. Prior to the 17th century, treacle was used medicinally to treat blood disorders. In old Ireland, sugar was expensive to buy and not readily available as a consequence. Treacle and honey were the only sweeteners for food, hence its popularity in the Irish kitchen. My great-grandmother, Cecily 'Handsome' Kearney, and my grandmother, Bridget McLaughlin, prepared their treacle bread on a griddle over the fire or sometimes baked it in a bastable pot – its lid covered in hot coals. Heston Blumenthal, in his book *Total Perfection*, mentions a 17th-century 'tart of bread' where treacle and bread are mixed with spices and dried fruit and baked in a pastry shell. I can attest that the concept still translates very well today – there's nothing like the smell of treacle bread wafting through the cottage on a winter's morning. Try this recipe, I think you'll love it – it's particularly delicious served with a wedge or two of good-quality butter.

*4⅔ cups (700g) self-raising (self-rising) flour, plus extra for dusting*

*3 cups (450g) wholemeal plain (all-purpose) flour*

*½ teaspoon sea salt flakes*

*2 teaspoons bicarbonate of (baking) soda*

*2½ teaspoons ground ginger*

*2 tablespoons finely chopped crystallised ginger*

*115g butter, chopped*

*⅓ cup (120g) treacle*

*¼ cup (90g) honey*

*2½ cups (625ml) buttermilk*

Preheat oven to 180°C (350°F). Lightly grease and flour a baking tray.

Sift the flours, salt, bicarbonate of soda and ground ginger into a large bowl and mix to combine. Add the crystallised ginger and mix to combine.

Place the butter, treacle and honey in a medium saucepan over medium heat and cook, stirring, until melted and smooth. Add the buttermilk and whisk to combine.

Add the treacle mixture to the flour mixture and mix into a sticky dough (there's no need to knead!). Turn the dough out directly onto the prepared tray and shape into an oval. Using a large knife that's been dipped in water then flour, cut a cross right over the bread, almost to the edges.

Bake for 15 minutes. Reduce the oven temperature to 150°C and bake for a further 40 minutes or until cooked through when tested with a knife. Watch the bread doesn't become too dark – if necessary, loosely cover with aluminium foil. Dust the bread lightly with flour to serve.

# biddy's SODA BREAD

*makes* 1 *large loaf*

Irish soda bread was born from poverty. It has always been associated
with the most basic of ingredients – flour, bread, soda, buttermilk and salt.
Butter and eggs were luxury goods and this basic bread mixture was cheap
to make (and, of course, filling). I grew up eating it. In fact, just out of the oven,
spread with melting butter and strawberry jam, it has to be one of my favourite
things. I can still see my mother in a snow storm of flour as she raised her arms
high to get the oxygen into it. I stood beside her, entranced. Marking the cross
on top of this wet and sticky dough was also a matter of great importance.
It's meant to ward off the devil and protect the family – in days gone by it was
done with great solemnity. This loaf is a particularly large one – Mum made it
every two days for her eight children and Dad. You can halve the recipe if you
prefer. Keep the bread for up to 1 week – it's gorgeous toasted.

6 cups (900g) strong (bread) plain (all-purpose) flour,
plus extra for dusting

2 teaspoons bicarbonate of (baking) soda

1½ teaspoons salt

2 tablespoons caster (superfine) sugar

2 eggs, lightly beaten

3⅓ cups (830ml) buttermilk

Preheat oven to 220°C (425°F). Line a large baking tray with
non-stick baking paper and dust with some extra flour.

Sift the flour and bicarbonate of soda from a height into a large bowl.
Add the salt and sugar and mix to combine with clean hands, lifting
and folding the mixture to let plenty of air in. Make a well in the centre.

Place the egg and buttermilk in a medium jug and whisk to combine.
Pour half the liquid into the well and use your fingers to rake the mixture
together. Repeat with the remaining liquid until a sticky dough forms.

Turn out the dough onto the prepared tray. Using clean hands that are
wet with a little warm water, shape the dough into a rough round. Wet
the back of a heavy knife, dip it in some extra flour and cut a cross incision
over the top of the dough. Reduce the oven temperature to 200°C (400°F)
and bake for 40–45 minutes, checking after 30 minutes to ensure the top
doesn't burn (reduce the oven temperature a little if it's looking dark).

Allow the bread to cool a little and serve warm with butter and jam.

*berleena's*

# PEA + HAM BREAD

*makes* 1 *small loaf*

Luckily for me, one of my best friends, Berleena, started her own business at about the same time as me. Ever since, we've been work buddies (and accountability partners!). She's a health coach and just as big of a foodie as me. We work together most days, taking it in turns to cook up a super healthy lunch. I'm always inspired by her new dishes and her approach to holistic living. Biddy fell in love with this bread when she tried it in Sydney. It's really tasty and packed to the brim with nourishing ingredients. You can check out more of Berleena's great recipes at *berleena.com*.

*1½ cups (180g) almond meal (ground almonds)*

*¾ cup (110g) arrowroot (tapioca flour)*

*½ teaspoon sea salt flakes*

*½ teaspoon bicarbonate of (baking) soda*

*½ cup (40g) finely grated parmesan*

*⅓ cup (55g) pepitas (pumpkin seeds)*

*1 tablespoon finely chopped rosemary or thyme leaves*

*½ cup (60g) frozen peas, thawed*

*120g sliced ham, chopped*

*5 eggs*

*1½ teaspoons apple cider vinegar*

Preheat oven to 180°C (350°F). Lightly grease a 10cm x 20cm loaf tin and line with non-stick baking paper.

Place the almond meal, arrowroot, salt and bicarbonate of soda in a large bowl. Add the parmesan and pepitas and mix to combine. Add the herbs, peas and ham and mix to combine.

Place the eggs and vinegar in a medium bowl and whisk to combine. Add to the pea and ham mixture and mix well.

Pour into the prepared tin and bake for 30 minutes or until golden on top and cooked when tested with a skewer.

Turn out of the tin and slice to serve warm, or allow to cool on a rack. This is delicious served with some herb butter.

# TRUDI'S *easy-peasy* PASTRY

*makes 1 pie base*

There is such an amazing Irish community in Australia and it has helped me so much with my business. I was lucky enough to meet Trudi at an Aisling Society dinner held in Sydney. We were at the same table and got chatting all about food. She told me amazing stories about growing up in Ireland and the food rituals they had. I knew I had to interview her for the book and so I went out to visit her in her home in Strathfield. When I was there she taught me how to make her famous quiche pastry. "Everyone in Strathfield knows this recipe", she told me. There's no rolling, no chilling butter for pastry, no blind baking, no hard work whatsoever! Plus you can use it for pies, too. It's genius and it's also delicious. I adore quiche, but it's usually a bit of a pain making one from scratch... not anymore! Thanks Trudi.

½ cup (125ml) milk

125g butter

2 cups (300g) self-raising (self-rising) flour

Place the milk and butter in a medium saucepan over medium heat, stirring, until melted and smooth. Allow to cool a little. I like to add the mixture to a bottle and run under a cold tap for a few minutes.

Add the flour and whisk to combine. Remove the pastry from the pan and shape into a round. Wrap in plastic wrap and refrigerate until ready to use, or simply use the pastry immediately.

———

NOTES – For extra flavour, you can add 1 teaspoon chopped rosemary leaves to the pan with the flour. See *recipes*, pages 101 and 103, for how to make this pastry into a pie and quiche.

———

GOD, Whose blessing we invoke upon our arms, and we pray that no one who serves
that cause will dishonour it by cowardice, inhumanity, or rapine. In this supreme
hour, the Irish nation must, by its valour and discipline and by the readiness of its
children to sacrifice themselves for the common good, prove itself worthy of the
august destiny to which it is called.

Signed on Behalf of the Provisional Government.

THOMAS J. CLARKE

SEAN Mac DIARMADA.          THOMAS MacDONAGH.

P. H. PEARSE.                    EAMONN CEANNT.

JAMES CONNOLLY.              JOSEPH PLUNKETT

and despised in many parts of Ireland. A Donegal crofter once told me he dare not keep a donkey for fear of being unable to marry off his daughters: instead he kept a horse, though he could ill afford one, for its prestige value. The dangerously monotonous diet of Irish countryfolk, also, can be explained in the light of the famine. So bitter is the folk-memory of these times that useful wild sources of food are now neglected and despised; for example, wild berries of all kinds, the ubiquitous eel, hare and rabbit; the cresses and the edible seaweeds and fungi. It should be added, however, that some of these foods were apparently tabu—the rabbit, an Anglo-Norman invader, was rarely eaten—and that the potato had played its part in debasing diet in the period before the famine.[1]

Perhaps the most striking example of reaction is to be found in the expressed desire of most country people to have an iso-lated dwelling-house. The clachan or hamlet, once the centre of communal life and tradition, is despised, a symbol of squabbling

[1] R. N. Salaman, *The History and Social Influence of the Potato* (1949), Ch.15.

11

A photograph of my great grandmother Cecily 'Handsome' Kearney (b.1860) and her 10-gallon black pot for boiling potatoes (left); An extract obtained from the Dept. of Folklore, U.C.D., Dublin (above).

Carrie Clancy, with Jack the donkey in Clonlara, Co Clare (main); and with her late husband David Clancy (above right).

# a tale of tea and the 'irish mammy'

My Nan, Carrie Clancy who lives in Clonlara, County Clare, has been one of the most inspirational people in my life. Beyond any doubt, my 'feeder' qualities have stemmed from her and I have so many fond food memories with her growing up. Whenever I arrive home from Sydney, I am relieved of all luggage, ushered into the kitchen, showered with big welcomes, ferocious hugs and tea... lots and lots of tea. The cycle starts at once. As soon as I am up, freshly baked chocolate croissants from the markets, perfectly brewed pots of Irish tea, bags and bags of Tayto crisps, fish pie for dinner. More tea. More goodies. Her fire lit in the corner of the living room all year round for me (I am constantly freezing arriving from sunny Bondi!).

Some of my favourite memories growing up include coming home to the mouth-watering smell of her weekly roast dinners, accompanied by the crispiest potatoes you can ever imagine. Trips into the *Curragower* restaurant for some delicious scampi and seafood chowder.

In her late thirties, she was given four days to live. However, her surgeon at the time told her to drink a glass of Guinness every day and the miracle is that she is still here – obviously the old marketing adage, "Guinness is good for you," has worked very well for her.

I remember she used to collect us from school, always regaling us with amusing stories and constructive suggestions about navigating life. When Biddy recently met Nan, she was taken aback by her speedy driving, quick wit and ferocious energy. Driving at 90 miles an hour, she landed us at the gate of her little menagerie of farm animals in just two minutes flat. We met Jack the donkey, Fudge the pony, the vigilant mammy goat and her triplets Dotty, Brownie and Ivan. "The pigs recognise the engine of my car," she smiles. "They are my buddies. They are pure pets."

Nan is a country woman whose life is synonymous with love and kindness. Biddy just loved her rhubarb tart and scoffed at least three slices, so we have an immense duty, we feel, to include her wonderful recipe on page 225. "Kady, you know I have baked two tarts every Sunday for the last forty years," she said, rolling out the finest pastry in her country kitchen. "I could make them with my eyes closed."

My Nan has been a massive influence on my life. Her kindness and quick wit can't help but leave you with a smile on your face. When my fiancé recently joked (during our Sunday Skype chat), that I wasn't ironing his shirts, she joked back to him with her trademark quick wit, "Ah now Niall...you don't buy a Ferrari and complain about the price of the fuel." That's Nan.

# SAUCES

+ CONDIMENTS

# CASHEW CREAM *with lemon zest*

*makes* ¾ cup

½ cup (75g) cashews

½ clove garlic, crushed

juice of ½ lemon

1 teaspoon finely grated lemon rind

1 tablespoon water

sea salt & cracked black pepper, to taste

Place all the ingredients in a blender and blend until smooth.

NOTE – Cashew cream is great with sweet potato fritters (see *recipe*, page 106).

---

# *blackcurrant* BRAMBLE

*makes* 1 cup

2 tablespoons water

1 tablespoon balsamic vinegar

½ teaspoon caster (superfine) sugar

250g blackcurrants

toasted flaked almonds, to serve

Place the water, vinegar and sugar in a medium saucepan over medium heat. Stir to dissolve the sugar and add the blackcurrants. Cook, stirring, for 5 minutes or until softened. Sprinkle with almonds to serve.

NOTE – Serve this tart-yet-sweet relish with the seared monkfish (see *recipe*, page 43) or with some marinated goat's cheese.

---

# *rustic* APPLE + THYME *sauce*

*makes* 1 cup

3 golden delicious apples or
2 small bramley apples (for a tart flavour)

¼ cup (55g) caster (superfine) sugar

1 teaspoon lemon juice

2 sprigs thyme, leaves picked

¾ cup (180ml) water

Peel the apples, remove the cores and chop them roughly. Place the apple, sugar, lemon juice, thyme and water in a medium saucepan over medium heat. Stir to combine. Bring to the boil, reduce the heat to low and simmer until soft. Roughly mash and set aside to cool. Refrigerate until chilled.

NOTES – This sauce will appear a little watery at first, but will set further on cooling. Serve with the pork schnitzel (see *recipe*, page 65).

# WALNUT SAUCE *with ginger cream*

*makes* 2 cups

1¾ cups (175g) walnuts, shelled

4 small cloves garlic

¾ cup (60g) finely grated pecorino

¾ cup (60g) finely grated parmesan

40g unsalted butter

⅓ cup (80ml) extra virgin olive oil

sea salt & cracked black pepper, to taste

⅓ cup (80ml) double (thick) cream

2 small pieces stem ginger, finely chopped

chopped sultanas (optional)

Preheat oven to 180°C (350°F). Spread the walnut halves in a single layer on a baking tray. Roast for 5–10 minutes or until dark and fragrant, turning a few times to prevent burning. Allow to cool on the tray.

Place the walnuts and garlic in a food processor and process until finely chopped. Add the cheeses, butter and oil and process into a paste.

Transfer the mixture to a bowl and season with salt and pepper. Add the cream and ginger, stir to combine and refrigerate until needed.

NOTE – This creamy sauce lasts up to 1 week in the fridge. It can be served hot or cold over pasta, and also makes a great dip! Try it with gnocchi (see *recipe*, page 121).

---

# *white* ONION VELOUTÉ

*makes* 2 cups

2 large white onions, finely chopped

1 clove garlic, finely chopped

50g butter

3 sprigs thyme

⅓ cup (50g) plain (all-purpose) flour

2 cups (500ml) vegetable or chicken stock

½ cup (125ml) double (thick) cream

sea salt & cracked black pepper, to taste

Place the onion, garlic, butter and thyme in a medium non-stick frying pan over medium heat. Cook, stirring, until very soft. Add the flour and stir until combined and bubbling. Gradually add the stock and cream, stirring constantly, until blended and smooth. Add salt and pepper to taste, then pass the sauce through a fine sieve, before serving.

NOTES – Most people serve this as a soup, and it is excellent. I also often use it as an unctuous, silky sauce, pairing it with a crunchy topping, like crispy slivers of garlic or pancetta. It's a gentle dish – the subtle flavours of the slow-cooked onions and garlic make it an ideal accompaniment to ham or chicken. You can try it with the slow-cooked pulled ham (see *recipe* page 59).

# bramley APPLE SAUCE with mint

*makes* 2 cup**s**

*1kg bramley apples (about 4 apples), peeled, cored and sliced*

*⅓ cup (75g) caster (superfine) sugar*

*⅓ cup (80ml) water*

*6 mint leaves, torn*

Place the apple, sugar and water in a large saucepan over medium heat. Slowly bring to the boil. Stir to combine and cover with a tight-fitting lid. Simmer for 5 minutes or until the apples become fluffy. Remove from the heat and allow to cool. Add the mint, mix to combine and serve warm or refrigerate until chilled.

NOTE – This is the quickest recipe ever. It takes minutes! Bramley sauce is the traditional accompaniment to roast pork, but I also love it with custard or mixed with both custard and cream to make old-fashioned apple fool. I usually have a big jar of apple sauce in the fridge as a standby for pancakes, yoghurt or ice-cream. It lasts up to 1 week or, if frozen, will keep for 6 months. Try it with our pear and pistachio stuffed pork (see *recipe*, page 57).

# stewed RHUBARB

*makes* 1 cup

*3 stalks rhubarb, chopped and leaves removed (they're poisonous!)*

*2 tablespoons maple syrup*

*1cm piece ginger, finely chopped*

*juice of 1 orange*

*2 tablespoons water*

Place the rhubarb, maple syrup, ginger, orange juice and water in a saucepan over medium heat and bring to the boil. Reduce the heat to low and simmer gently for 5–7 minutes or until soft.

NOTE – Serve this tart compote with our nutty granola (see *recipe*, page 16).

# marinated LABNE

*makes* 8-10 *balls*

2⅔ cups (750g) plain greek-style (thick) yoghurt

1 teaspoon sea salt flakes

1 cup (250ml) extra virgin olive oil

1 sprig rosemary

1 tablespoon finely chopped flat-leaf parsley leaves

finely grated rind of ½ lemon

Place the yoghurt and salt in a large bowl and mix to combine.

Line a sieve with clean muslin or cheesecloth and set it over a bowl. Add the yoghurt mixture and gather up the edges of the muslin to enclose, securing with string. Place in the fridge and allow to drain for 3 days.

Discard the liquid in the bowl. Roll tablespoons of the labne into balls and place on a tray. Refrigerate for 1 hour or until set. Place the labne balls in a sterilised jar and top with the oil, herbs and lemon rind. Keep in the fridge for up to 1 week.

NOTES – Labne is delicious mixed into any salad. It's also used in the whiskey cloud cake (see *recipe*, page 230), just skip out on the oil and herbs.

---

# biddy's BREAD SAUCE

*makes* 3 cups

8 whole cloves

1 medium onion, peeled

2 cups (500ml) milk

4 cups (280g) white breadcrumbs

1 pinch nutmeg

sea salt & cracked white pepper, to taste

Press the cloves into the onion. Place in a medium saucepan, add the milk and simmer over medium heat for 15 minutes or until soft.

Remove and discard the onion and cloves with a slotted spoon. Add the breadcrumbs, nutmeg and a little salt and pepper and mix well to combine.

NOTE – Serve bread sauce with your favourite roast. It's especially good with the crispy bacon roasted partridges (see *recipe*, page 258).

# *sweetie sharpy* SALAD DRESSING

*makes ½ cup*

¼ cup (60ml) extra virgin olive oil

1½ tablespoons white balsamic vinegar

1½ tablespoons lime juice

½ teaspoon dijon mustard

1 pinch sea salt flakes

8 basil leaves

Place all the ingredients in a blender and blend until smooth and combined.

NOTE – This dressing goes beautifully with the pulled ham crock pot with pear salad (see *recipe*, page 59).

---

# *crystallised* LEMON RIND

*makes* 2 cup**s**

4 large unwaxed lemons, halved and peeled, rind sliced into long thin strips

2 cups (440g) white (granulated) sugar

Place the rind strips in a saucepan of boiling water over high heat. Return to the boil and cook for 30 seconds. Drain. Repeat this process, cooking for a full 1 minute this time, and drain the rind (this step helps to remove bitterness and increase tenderness in the rind).

Place 1¾ cups (385g) of the sugar in a medium saucepan and cover with 1¾ cups (430ml) cold water. Bring to the boil over medium heat, stirring to dissolve the sugar. When the syrup is thick, add the lemon rind. Remove from the heat and set aside for 10 minutes. Sprinkle half the remaining ¼ cup sugar (55g) onto a large sheet of non-stick baking paper. Remove the rind from the syrup, using a slotted spoon, and place it on the paper. Sprinkle the last of the sugar on top. Cover loosely with aluminium foil and allow to stand at room temperature for 6 hours or overnight.

Cut the strips into 5mm pieces and place in a sterilised jar. Seal with a tight-fitting lid and keep at room temperature for up to 2 months.

NOTE – Serve with our best-ever lemon spaghetti (see *recipe*, page 77).

# the decline of
## *afternoon tea*

*The makings of our Banana and Nutella cake with Salted Caramel.*

For me, afternoon tea is all about good taste. It has to be fancy and should include tiers of the requisite crustless finger sandwiches of smoked salmon, roast ham or beef, cucumber or egg and chive fingers, fresh raisin scones with Cornish clotted cream and strawberry jam. Afternoon tea is all about delicate delights, a slim slice of homemade Battenberg, a proper cream eclair, an iced fancy or a delicate piece of Victoria sponge. Each tiny morsel that enters your mouth should be pure heaven.

Serving tea is a ceremonial occasion. It should be slightly formal, cosy and comfortable, preferably imbibed around a sturdy fire. Elegant, sumptuous food, good company and of course great gossip, should be the only criterion. It is typically served from 3pm to 6pm.

These days afternoon tea has gone to pot. Recently I brought my little niece Kate, for a treat, to a well known hotel in Dublin. As we hurtled our way on the Dart to Pearse St. Station, I regaled her with stories of bone china cups, of smoky Earl Grey tea, cream puffs that were so light they melted in your mouth. And definitely we were going to have a cucumber slice or two!

Instead we were presented with a savoury slice of chorizo, onion and thyme Wellington slice, a roll filled with diced boar and mustard topped with a dab of pickled apple and tiny crackling pork pieces. Some stalks of miniature celery with coriander crowns were standing in a glass jar. Kate sat silently and stared. The array of sweets was visually extraordinary but oh the taste! It was dire. Bubblegum sponge, lemon and pistachio marshmallows and then a production line of gloopy mousses in shot glasses. Great for babies with no teeth – salted caramel mousse, dark chocolate mousse, pistachio pot cream, a sour cream mousse, some with a light sprinkle of gold leaf and chia seed dust, dried and tautened by gelatine.

Hey, where is the cake? We were longing for a little slice of Mary Berry's homemade Battenberg, a proper cream eclair that was NOT filled with mango mousse!, an elegant iced fancy, decent fresh raisin scones that didn't crumble like sawdust after being defrosted in the microwave. Good old-fashioned afternoon tea? I think not.

Afternoon tea, once a lovely tradition has become performance art. Pastry chefs have complicated every aspect of their presentations. There are so many new trends it is hard to keep up. 'Cake and cocktail' pairing. Hmm. Hotels are serving cocktails per cake, in the hope that you get so drunk you'll forget the whole experience. The Shelbourne Hotel has afternoon tea paired with the paintings by Michael Flatley, Lord of the Dance, and a dear friend of mine. "The pastry team's own artistic impulses have been triggered by the colours, textures and themes of his paintings to create desserts inspired by Elvis, Playful, The Grand National and Nella Fantasia."

Surely we are losing the plot? Michael is one of the most talented people I know but I blame hotel management and the chefs who really need to get a grip on themselves. As my father would say, afternoon tea is now "all pipe, no tobaccy." I heartily wish we could just revert to the tradition and elegance of a classic afternoon tea. Thank God for people like Mary Berry keeping the classics alive!

CKS + NIBBLES

*biddy's ginger*
# OATCAKES

*makes* 30

Oats, despite our obsession with potato, were the mainstay of the pre-potato Irish diet. My father remembers his grandmother Cecily 'Handsome' Kearney (CHK) cooking oats in a traditional Donegal way... mixing them with boiling water and butter in a big bowl, then flattening the mixture onto the top of a wooden milk churn where it would harden outside of the house for most of the day. Later she would lift this enormous hard 'cookie' and place it on the three-legged Harnen stand or oat toaster to bake in front of the turf fire until golden. The secret to divine oatcakes, I have found, is as old as the hills, but Good Lord it ain't easy. "Two pieces of oatcake and a drop of buttermilk sustained you for the whole day," my Dad told me. So, I spent the guts of a year trying to recreate his description of them using everything from pinhead oatmeal to oatmeal flakes. It was, I can honestly say, the most rewarding task ever. I even sourced and bought an 18th century Irish Harnen stand for myself. If you are going to attempt CHK's very own recipe, I recommend you use oat 'groats' (the whole grain kernel). I won't lie, these oatcakes are tricky and you need the patience of Job, but wow are they worth it.
Top tip – don't take your eye off the oatcakes in the oven, they burn easily.

*1kg whole oat groates*

*½ cup (75g) plain (all-purpose) flour*

*½ cup (110g) white (granulated) sugar*

*2 teaspoons sea salt flakes*

*3 teaspoons ground ginger*

*½ cup (50g) finely chopped crystallised ginger*

*85g butter, chopped*

*½ cup (118ml) boiling water*

Preheat oven to 200°C (400°F). Lightly grease 2 bakings trays.

Place the oat groates, flour, sugar, salt and the ground and crystallised ginger in a large bowl. Mix to combine.

Place the butter in a small saucepan over medium heat until melted and bubbling. Add the boiling water and mix well. Immediately add the butter mixture to the dry ingredients and, working quickly, mix to combine.

Place a 5cm cutter down on 1 of the trays and press 1 tablespoon of the mixture inside to shape, pressing gently with the back of a teaspoon. Remove the cutter and repeat with the remaining mixture and tray, leaving room for the oatcakes to spread a little.

Place the trays in the middle of the oven and bake for 25 minutes or until golden. Allow to cool on the trays and store for up to 1 month in an airtight container.

# DIY *open* SAMBOS

*makes* **2** *of each*

You can't go wrong with a good old sambo. Quick and easy to make, these fillings will inspire you to shake up your regular lunch staple. Use treacle bread (see *recipe*, page 167) or soda bread (see *recipe*, page 169), fresh or toasted.

### EGG + MAYO

*4 free-range eggs*

*2–3 tablespoons whole-egg mayonnaise*

*1 green onion (scallion), trimmed and chopped*

*sea salt & cracked black pepper, to taste*

*butter, for spreading*

*2 slices bread*

### PICKLED CUCUMBER

*1 tablespoon whole-egg mayonnaise*

*2 slices bread, toasted*

*1 pickled cucumber, sliced*

*1 tablespoon finely grated parmesan*

*1 tablespoon chopped dill sprigs*

### TUNA PESTO

*1 x 100g can tuna, drained*

*3 tablespoons sundried tomato pesto*

*2 slices bread, toasted*

*½ red onion, finely chopped*

*6 semi-sundried tomatoes*

*2 tablespoons crumbled feta*

### HAM + PINEAPPLE CHUTNEY

*2 slices bread*

*butter, for spreading*

*2 slices ham (40g)*

*2 tablespoons store-bought pineapple chutney*

### EGG + MAYO

Place the eggs in a saucepan of cold water over medium heat and bring to the boil. Boil for 5 minutes. Drain the eggs and run them under cold water. Crack and peel away the shells and place the eggs in a medium bowl. Mash with a fork and add the mayo, onion, salt and pepper and mix. Spread each slice of bread with butter and top with the egg mix.

### PICKLED CUCUMBER

Spread the mayo on 2 slices of the toast. Top with the pickles, parmesan and dill.

### TUNA PESTO

Place the tuna and pesto in a small bowl and mix to combine. Spread onto 2 slices of the toast and top with the onion, tomatoes and feta.

### HAM + PINEAPPLE CHUTNEY

Spread each slice of bread with butter. Top 2 of the slices with the ham and pineapple chutney.

# sugar-free NUTTY CHOCOLATE bites

*makes 8–10*

As Biddy and I were working away on this part of the book in her cottage, measuring flour and stirring in sugar, the smells of our baking would waft out onto the windy roads of Dalkey, outside the half door. There were many a visitor. Every day, Biddy's sister Nibs (who happens to be diabetic) would pop her head in. I would feel awful as she watched us taste our recipes in silent appreciation. We would be taking a tea break with cakes laid out before us, some cookies standing to cool on the counter top. I remembered when I did a sugar/gluten/alcohol-free detox in Sydney and the daily struggle that was, for 4 weeks. I am a huge snacker with a serious sweet tooth so I had to find a treat that was sneakily sugar-free yet delicious… and I did after countless experiments. I made some for Nibs and they got her tick of approval, so these are dedicated to her!

*1 tablespoon crunchy peanut butter*

*1 heaped teaspoon lucuma powder*

*2 heaped tablespoons raw cacao powder, plus extra for dusting*

*2 teaspoons vanilla powder*

*1 tablespoon almond meal (ground almonds)*

*⅓ cup (80ml) almond milk*

*1 tablespoon shredded coconut*

*2 drops liquid stevia*
*(you can use 1 teaspoon honey if you can tolerate sugar)*

*1 pinch sea salt flakes*

*1 tablespoon cacao nibs or goji berries*

Place all the ingredients in a large bowl and mix well to combine.

Roll 1 tablespoon of the mixture into a ball and place on a tray. Repeat with the remaining mixture, and refrigerate until chilled.

Dust the bites with a little extra cacao powder, if you like, and store in an airtight container in the fridge for up to 1 week.

———

NOTE – You'll find most of these ingredients in the health-food aisle of the supermarket or from health food shops. I also love *iherb.com*.

# JAIME'S *epic* COOKIES
## *with a twist of* ROSEMARY

*serves* 10–12

My sister, Jaime, loved to bake when we were growing up. I would always beg her to make cookies or brownies and promise to do all of the dishes after her in return. She's been making these cookies for years and they are so delicious. They're the perfect combination of crunchy and chewy, which is vital in a good cookie. The key is to put the mix in the fridge before baking.

A couple of days a week, I work with my friend Berleena, who started her business around the same time as me. It's so great to have her support and, better still, she's a foodie like me. One day Berleena had made healthy dark chocolate and rosemary cookies and I was blown away by what an amazing flavour combination it was. Having the sweet tooth that I do, I tried this combo out on my 'not-so-healthy' cookies and... oh my goodness! It's divine. I've been making them like this ever since and they're always a huge hit.

225g butter, chopped

3–4 sprigs rosemary, leaves chopped

½ cup (110g) caster (superfine) sugar

½ cup (90g) brown sugar

1 egg yolk

½ teaspoon vanilla extract

2 cups (300g) plain (all-purpose) flour, plus extra for dusting

1 teaspoon baking powder

250g dark chocolate chips

Place the butter and rosemary in a small saucepan over low heat until melted. Transfer to a large bowl and set aside to cool for 10 minutes. Add both the sugars to the rosemary butter and beat, using an electric mixer, until pale and fluffy. Add the egg yolk and vanilla and beat to combine. Sift in the flour and baking powder and fold to combine. Add the chocolate chips and fold to combine.

Sprinkle some extra flour on a clean, dry benchtop and roll the dough out into a long log. Wrap the dough in plastic wrap and refrigerate for at least 1 hour.

Preheat oven to 180°C (350°F). Unwrap the dough and slice into 3cm-thick rounds. Place on a baking tray lined with non-stick baking paper (leaving room for the cookies to spread) and bake for 15 minutes or until golden. Allow to cool on the trays.

# ZUCCHINI *scrolls*

*makes* 30

I absolutely adore having friends over and throwing dinner parties. I do it all the time and it's a great excuse to make fun finger food like this. Food, to me, is what brings people together and I love any excuse to do just that. These scrolls are delicious little bites that seem to disappear very quickly anytime they are made. Enjoy!

*1 tablespoon extra virgin olive oil*

*1 large zucchini (courgette), thinly sliced with a mandolin*

*sea salt & cracked black pepper, to taste*

*⅓ cup (90g) pesto*

*85g goat's cheese*

Preheat oven to 180°C (350°F). Line a baking tray with non-stick baking paper and brush it lightly with the oil.

Arrange the strips of zucchini flat on the tray and sprinkle with salt and pepper. Roast for 5 minutes until just soft. Allow to cool. Spoon about ½ teaspoon pesto and ½ teaspoon goat's cheese over each strip of zucchini and roll into a scroll. Place upright on a serving platter and serve.

# *fudgy* VANILLA
# + ALMOND *cookies*

*makes* 8

I love to experiment with dairy, gluten and sugar-free recipes. And because I like to bake so much, it's great to have a few recipes up my sleeve that are actually healthy. However, one thing I will never sacrifice is taste, so all of these creations have to taste just as good, if not better, than the real deal. These cookies do just that! They are fudgy and chewy with a buttery smooth vanilla centre. Absolutely delicious as an afternoon treat.

*1 cup (120g) almond meal (ground almonds)*

*½ cup (80g) organic coconut sugar*

*½ teaspoon vanilla bean paste*

*1 egg, separated*

*1 teaspoon honey*

*1 pinch sea salt flakes*

*1 tablespoon water*

*shredded coconut (optional), to serve*

*lavender petals (optional), to serve*

Place the almond meal, sugar, vanilla, egg white, honey and salt in a large bowl and mix well to combine. Turn the dough out and roll into a log. Wrap in plastic wrap and freeze for 2 hours.

Preheat oven to 180°C (350°F). Line a baking tray with non-stick baking paper.

Remove the dough from the freezer and unwrap. Cut into 1cm-thick slices and place on the prepared tray, leaving room for the cookies to spread a little.

Place the egg yolk in a small bowl and mix with the water. Brush over the surface of the cookies.

Bake for 25 minutes or until golden. Allow to cool on the tray. Top with the coconut and lavender to serve.

# balsamic STRAWBERRY bites

*makes 48*

When I lived in Vancouver, I worked in an amazing restaurant that had about 7 sister restaurants all around the city. They really encouraged you to go and try the other restaurants. I brought my sister in to one of them for a 7-course tasting meal when she came to visit and it was out of this world. One dish that has aways stuck with me was the strawberries, stuffed with goat's cheese and balsamic vinegar, that came out before the entree. So simple, but such an unusual and delicious pairing of flavours.

*75g soft goat's cheese*

*500g strawberries, hulled and halved*

*small mint leaves, to serve*

*balsamic vinegar reduction, to serve*

Spoon a little goat's cheese onto each strawberry half.
Top with a mint leaf and place on a serving platter. Drizzle with
the balsamic reduction to serve. Watch them disappear!

# *ballymaloe* RELISH + GOAT'S CHEESE *tarts*

*serves* 4

*Ballymaloe relish* is, in my opinion, one of the most precious exports of Ireland. My fiancé is so obsessed with it, he has my grandmother posting it to him in Australia (even though it is available here!). We always spread it on sandwiches and wraps, but one day I decided to use it as a base for a puff pastry slice and it was incredible. The relish caramelises into the pastry and, combined with red onion and goat's cheese, is the definition of 'moreish'.

*⅓ cup (90g) ballymaloe original relish or tomato relish*

*1 sheet ready-rolled puff pastry, cut into 4 rectangles*

*¼ red onion, thinly sliced*

*50g marinated goat's feta, crumbled*

Preheat oven to 200°C (400°F).

Spread 1 tablespoon of the relish onto each piece of pastry. Top with the onion and feta.

Place on a baking tray and bake for 15–20 minutes or until golden and caramelised.

———

NOTE – For my fellow Australian residents, you'll find *Ballymaloe original relish* and all the other Irish products you need at *tasteireland.com.au*

For extra recipe ideas, I also do a weekly guest post on *tasteireland.com.au/kadys-kitchen*

———

W hen I saw my eagerly awaited 'panna cotta', en route to my table, I sighed. It looked lonely, sad and ever so grey, naked, in the middle of its enormous white ceramic dish, a heavy drizzle of processed raspberry coulis its only friend. I looked at it and it looked back at me – neither wanting introductions. A real dessert should uplift one's soul, its taste and colour, partners in crime. This had neither.

Rebelling at the sight, I perused the menu for a second time. The usual suspects were out in force – a creme brûlée, a brownie with ice-cream, a slice of banoffee, a slice of cheesecake, a slice of weary apple tart – all bought-in confections made to a time-starved commercial recipe of endless ingredients with ne'er a pastry chef in sight.

I gambled on the cheescake, for old time's sake, and was presented with a philadelphia gelatine mix sitting on a rather unattractive layer of damp biscuit concrete – dressed in the finery of a furry kiwi. Who knew?

A little lemon meringue pie, perhaps?

I stared at the ashen faced waiter as he arrived with his next offering – a shiny wedge of lemony something, canary yellow in colour. Its once snowy peaks were blow-torched into submission, and I can attest without any fear of contradiction that it was possibly the worst dessert I had ever eaten. That was, until my friend proffered a tablespoon of his Eton mess. This Eton mess was the most dire of all the desserts. It was what it said it was. A mess. A lazy chef's way of shoving everything into a glass, topping it with aerosol cream, some notorious 'coulis' and flinging it over his shoulder from the kitchen.

I find that Ireland is utterly remarkable for its lack of imaginative desserts. Kady and I hope that this book will remedy this national oversight by including our loved, pre-loved and ever loved desserts with Kady's top dog and show stopper, the Whiskey Cloud Cake... now you're talking!

*dessert menu*

# DESSERTS

# BANANA + NUTELLA *cake* *with* SALTED CARAMEL

*serves* 8–10

Baking a cake for someone you adore is one of the most special things. For birthdays especially – they're my favourite present to give. I love dreaming up signature cakes for my friends – tailoring their cake to match them, using their most loved sweet treats and flavours. This particular cake is super indulgent. It's a little chewy, with smooth swirls of banana and Nutella, topped with salted caramel. A true crowd pleaser.

*4 medium ripe bananas, plus extra, sliced, to serve*

*100g butter, chopped*

*1 cup (150g) plain (all-purpose) flour*

*1 pinch sea salt flakes*

*1 teaspoon baking powder*

*1 teaspoon bicarbonate of (baking) soda*

*¾ cup (135g) light brown sugar*

*2 eggs*

*½ teaspoon vanilla extract*

*¼ cup (60ml) milk*

*⅓ cup (110g) nutella*

## SALTED CARAMEL

*80g butter*

*1 cup (175g) light brown sugar*

*¼ cup (60ml) boiling water*

*¼ cup (60ml) single (pouring) cream*

*1 teaspoon vanilla extract*

*1 teaspoon sea salt flakes*

Preheat oven to 180°C (350°F). Lightly grease a 20cm round cake tin and line it with non-stick baking paper.

Place the bananas in a large bowl and mash until almost smooth. Add the butter, flour, salt, baking powder, bicarbonate of soda, sugar, eggs and vanilla. Mix well to combine and set aside. Place the milk and Nutella in a small saucepan over low heat until melted and smooth. Add the Nutella mixture to the cake mixture, gently folding to combine to create a marbled effect. Pour the mixture into the prepared tin and bake for 30–40 minutes or until cooked when tested with a skewer. Turn the cake out onto a wire rack to cool.

To make the salted caramel, place the butter, sugar and water in a small saucepan over medium heat and bring to a gentle boil until the sugar is dissolved. Add the cream, vanilla and salt and whisk to combine. Bring to a steady simmer for 3 minutes until the sauce is sticky and thick. Set aside to cool slightly.

Place the cake on a serving plate or cake stand and pour over the salted caramel. Top with the extra banana.

NOTE – If your bananas are not very ripe, you can place them in a hot oven for 5 minutes or until the skin turns black. You can caramelise the extra banana slices for the top of the cake by sautéing them for 2–3 minutes in 1 teaspoon of butter in a non-stick frying pan.

# *nell's* APPLE TART

*serves 6–8*

When I asked Nell Fitzgerald, of Juggy's Well restaurant in Glasthule, could we include her apple tart for our book, she made no objection of any sort. That's the kind of woman she is. I don't think it's possible to taste a better tart than Nell's. Every morning, there's a queue from the door of her restaurant to the counter, all dying for a slice of her signature bake. The pastry is golden, flaky and light. The apples are tart – not too much sugar. Occasionally in the last few years I've dropped into her tiny kingdom, a simple kitchen corner of the restaurant, to observe this master baker at work. There's an enchanting liveliness to the chats and craic, but she puts a great deal of thought into her method. "The rule of thumb for any pastry is half fat to 1kg of flour," she says, her hair covered in a fine dust of flour. "I need to remind you of the ground rules, Biddy… don't forget this is a 'large' tart. Don't eat it all yourself!"

4½ cups (675g) plain (all-purpose) flour, plus extra for dusting

½ teaspoon sea salt flakes

345g vegetable shortening, chopped and at room temperature
(try brands like copha, stork or cookeen)

2 eggs, lightly beaten, plus 1 extra for brushing

1¼ cups (310ml) cold water

4 medium bramley apples (1kg), peeled cored and thinly sliced

¾ cup (165g) white (granulated) sugar, plus extra for sprinkling

Sift the flour and salt into a large bowl. Add the vegetable shortening and, using your fingertips, rub it into the flour until the mixture resembles fine breadcrumbs. Add the eggs and a little of the water and knead gently until a soft dough comes together, adding more water if necessary.

Roll the dough out onto a clean surface dusted lightly in flour. Fold the bottom half of the dough up to the centre, and the top over to the base. Repeat this step three more times.

Wrap the dough in plastic wrap. Refrigerate for 1 hour.

Preheat oven to 190°C (375°F). Lightly grease a 25cm round pie dish or ovenproof plate.

Divide the chilled dough in half and, on a clean surface dusted lightly in flour, roll one of the pieces out into a circle that's just larger than your pie dish.

Transfer the pastry to line the pie dish and trim the edges with a small sharp knife. Arrange the apple slices on top and sprinkle evenly with the sugar. Brush the edges of the pastry with a little of the extra egg.

Roll out the remaining dough into a round that's a little larger than the top of the dish. Use it to cover the apples. Trim to fit and pinch the edges to seal the tart. Use a fork or your fingers to mark the edges.

Slice a cross in the centre of the pastry or prick it in several places with a fork. Brush the entire surface with extra egg. Sprinkle with extra sugar.

Bake the tart, on the top shelf of the oven, for 15 minutes. Reduce the oven temperature to 170°C (340°F), move the tart to the middle shelf and bake for a further 30 minutes or until cooked through and golden.

# BLACKBERRY +
## *blue cheese* GALETTE

*serves* 2–4

Biddy and I were walking through the woods one day with
Bill 'the mushroom man' O'Dea, foraging for mushrooms. I was telling
Biddy about how odd my taste buds are and laughing that there was
no food in the fridge earlier, so I'd baked blackberries and blue cheese in a
ramekin and ate it with a fork! To my surprise, Biddy and Bill loved the idea.
With a little extra reassurance from them, I set about developing my
accidental creation into a proper recipe, and this galette was born.
It's the ultimate dessert really... a cheese plate and fruit tart all in one!

1¼ cups (200g) plain (all-purpose) flour

½ teaspoon sea salt flakes

120g cold butter, chopped

¼ cup (60ml) iced water

¼ cup (60g) sour cream

2 teaspoons lemon juice

1 cup (125g) blackberries

75g blue cheese, crumbled

1 teaspoon brown sugar

1 egg, lightly beaten

Sift the flour and salt into a large bowl. Add the butter and, using your
fingertips, rub together until the mixture resembles breadcrumbs. Set aside.

Place the water, sour cream and lemon juice in a small bowl and mix to
combine. Add to the butter mixture and stir until just combined. Turn out
the mixture onto a sheet of plastic wrap and form it into a ball of dough
as you enclose. Refrigerate for at least 1 hour (or for up to 2 days).

Preheat oven to 180°C (350°F). Remove the dough from the fridge,
unwrap it and place it between two sheets of non-stick baking paper.
Roll out the dough into a rough round. Transfer the pastry onto a baking
tray and peel off the top sheet of paper. Top the pastry with the blackberries
and cheese, leaving a 2cm border. Fold the edges of the pastry up to
enclose the filling. Sprinkle with the sugar and brush the edges with
egg. Bake for 35 minutes or until golden.

*the cheating chef's*

# RASPBERRY CHEESECAKE

*serves* 2

Cheat your way to these gorgeous individual desserts – they look as if they were conceived in a Parisian patisserie. Easy to prep ahead of time, make two for a special romantic dessert, or increase the recipe for a sweets table or high tea. But shhh! Don't tell your impressed guests the simple secret.

*250g mascarpone*

*¼ cup (55g) caster (superfine) sugar*

*juice and finely grated rind of 1 lemon*

*300g raspberries*

*2 mcvitie's digestive biscuits or plain sweet wheat biscuits*

*1 tablespoon desiccated coconut or icing (confectioner's) sugar*

Place the mascarpone in a medium bowl and add the sugar, lemon rind and juice and 6 of the raspberries. Gently fold to combine.

Place 1 biscuit at the base of each of 2 x 7cm round loose-based mousse moulds. Divide the mascarpone mixture between the moulds, spreading to fill, and refrigerate the cakes for 1 hour.

Remove the cakes from the fridge 5 minutes before serving and carefully run a knife around the inside of the moulds. Gently push the bases up and place the cakes onto serving plates. Top each with a tower of the remaining raspberries and sprinkle with the coconut to serve.

# gooseberry FOOL

*serves 4*

There's nothing quite so delicious as good old-fashioned Gooseberry Fool.
I associate it with my childhood in North County Dublin, where there was always
a glut of gooseberries in June and July. I remember my mother
folding the chilled stewed gooseberries into sweet cold custard, then hearing
the soft plop of thick whipped cream as she swirled it through the smooth
vanilla custard with her wooden spoon. My finger was first in. And the taste,
oh my goodness – the milky, creamy undertones of the sweet and tart
flavours changing was pure heaven. Don't forget, the real tangy taste of
gooseberries lies in the skin (so it's best not to sieve them). This beautiful
homemade custard recipe was given to us by our dear friend Berleena
– it's the perfect modern addition to a classic.

1⅓ cups (275g) gooseberries

⅓ cup (75g) caster (superfine) sugar

½ cup (125ml) water

**CUSTARD**

2 cups (500ml) milk or coconut milk

1 pinch nutmeg

1 teaspoon vanilla powder

2 tablespoons maple syrup or 1 tablespoon honey

4 egg yolks

2 tablespoons cornflour (cornstarch)
or arrowroot (tapioca flour)

2 tablespoons brandy or bourbon whiskey

sea salt flakes, to taste

Place the gooseberries, sugar and water in a medium saucepan over medium heat and cook,
stirring, for 5 minutes or until a little swollen. Set aside to cool.

To make the custard, place the milk, nutmeg, vanilla and maple in a medium saucepan over
medium heat. Bring just to the boil, remove from the heat and set aside. Place the egg yolks
and cornflour in a medium bowl (I find this works best in a metal mixing bowl) and whisk until
smooth. Very gradually pour the hot milk into the egg mixture, whisking constantly, until combined.
Pour the mixture back into the saucepan and place over low heat. Cook, stirring, for 3–5 minutes
or until thickened. Add the brandy and a little salt, stir to combine and remove from the heat.

Divide between serving bowls and top with the stewed gooseberries.

NOTE – You can, of course, use classic or store-bought custard for this recipe, too. For extra lightness,
add 2–3 tablespoons of whipped cream and fold to combine before adding the stewed gooseberries.

# RHUBARB TART

*serves 6–8*

My grandmother has been making this tart for decades. In fact, she makes two every Sunday. When I ask her what for, she tells me "for whoever stops by during the week". She always has people in and out and they enjoy a special slice with her over a cup of tea. I think this is such a beautiful tradition and something to treasure in our fast-paced lives. It's from rituals like this that Irish people get their reputations for being such wonderful hosts and so caring. The true 'Irish Mammy' in action!

¾ cup (110g) plain (all-purpose) flour

90g margarine or butter, chopped and softened

60g vegetable shortening, chopped and softened (try brands like copha, stork or cookeen)

2 tablespoons cold water

1 egg, lightly beaten

## RHUBARB FILLING

2 ¼ cups (500g) caster (superfine) sugar

½ cup (125ml) water

5–6 stalks rhubarb, chopped and leaves removed (they're poisonous!)

To make the rhubarb filling, place the sugar, water and rhubarb in a large saucepan over medium heat and bring to the boil. Allow to simmer for 5 minutes. Set aside to cool.

Place the flour in a large bowl and add the margarine and vegetable shortening. Using your fingertips, rub the mixture together until it resembles breadcrumbs. Add the chilled water and knead gently until a soft dough forms, adding more water if necessary. Wrap the dough in plastic wrap and refrigerate for 1 hour or overnight.

Preheat oven to 230°C (445°F). Lightly grease a 25cm round pie dish or ovenproof plate.

Divide the chilled dough in half and, on a clean surface dusted lightly in flour, roll 1 of the pieces out into a circle that's just larger than your pie dish.

Transfer the pastry to line the pie dish and trim the edges with a small sharp knife. Top with the stewed rhubarb. Brush the edges of the pastry with the egg.

Roll out the remaining dough into a round that's a little larger than the top of the dish, and use it to cover the rhubarb. Trim to fit and pinch the edges to seal the tart. Brush the top of the tart with egg and use the tines of a fork to pierce the pastry all over. Bake for 30 minutes or until crisp and golden. Slice and serve warm or chill and serve cold.

NOTE – Lard or butter can be used instead of vegetable shortening.

*sticky* APRICOT, ORANGE *and date* PUDDING

*serves* 6–8

Is there anything quite so tempting as a bowl of dark sticky toffee pudding smothered in caramel? This recipe uses apricots and orange with the dates which gives a lovely extra dimension of flavour. Rich and indulgent, this is a cosy, comforting dessert that everyone loves.

### SALTED CARAMEL

80g butter

1 cup (175g) light brown sugar

¼ cup (60ml) boiling water

¼ cup (60ml) single (pouring) cream

1 teaspoon vanilla extract

1 teaspoon sea salt flakes

juice of ½ lemon

1 cup (140g) dried pitted dates

¾ cup (100g) dried apricots

1½ cups (375ml) water

2 teaspoons bicarbonate of (baking) soda

⅓ cup (55g) almonds

100g butter, chopped and softened

1¼ cups (220g) brown sugar

3 eggs

finely grated rind and juice of ½ orange

1⅔ cups (250g) plain (all-purpose) flour, sifted

Preheat oven to 180°C (350°F). Lightly grease a 24cm round cake tin and line with non-stick baking paper.

To make the salted caramel, place the butter, sugar and water in a small saucepan over medium heat and bring to a gentle boil, stirring until the sugar is dissolved. Add the cream, vanilla and salt and whisk to combine. Bring to a steady simmer for 3 minutes or until the sauce is sticky and thick. Add the lemon juice and whisk to combine. Measure ¾ cup (180ml) of the sauce and pour it into the prepared tin.

Place the dates and apricots in a food processor and process until chopped. Transfer to a medium saucepan over medium heat and add the water and bicarbonate of soda. Bring to the boil, reduce the heat to low and simmer until the fruit is soft. Set aside to cool.

Place the almonds on a baking tray and roast for 10 minutes or until lightly toasted, checking occasionally to ensure they don't burn.

Place the butter and sugar in a large bowl and beat, using an electric mixer, until pale and fluffy. Add the eggs, 1 at a time, beating between each addition. Add the date mixture, orange juice, orange rind and toasted almonds to the butter mixture and stir to combine. Add the flour and fold until just smooth and combined.

Pour the mixture into the prepared tin and bake for 45 minutes or until cooked when tested with a skewer. Heat the remaining sauce and pour it over slices of the pudding to serve.

# whiskey CLOUD CAKE

*serves 6—8*

Made with labne (yoghurt cheese), this cheesecake has a slightly tangy
flavour which the smoky whiskey-honey glaze complements perfectly. When
we finished shooting it for this book, Biddy and I both sprawled out on her
couch in the cottage, cups of tea in hand, and ate it in silent appreciation.
Dishes and platters of food scattered all around us from a long day's work,
we sat in pure joy devouring this fluffy, heavenly cake. You can make your
own homemade labne (see *recipe*, page 185) or buy it at all good delis.

### CHEESECAKE BASE

*175g pecans*

*50g butter, melted*

*sea salt flakes, to taste*

### FILLING

*225g labne (see recipe, page 185)
or well-drained cottage cheese*

*3 free-range eggs, separated*

*¾ cup (210g) plain greek-style (thick) yoghurt*

*½ cup (110g) caster (superfine) sugar*

*8 pecans, for decorating*

### WHISKEY-HONEY GLAZE

*½ cup (180g) raw honey*

*2 tablespoons good-quality bourbon whiskey*

*1 tablespoon lemon juice*

*½ teaspoon sea salt flakes*

Preheat oven to 160°C (325°F). Lightly grease a 20cm round springform cake tin and line with non-stick
baking paper.

To make the cheesecake base, place the pecans in a food processor and process until they
resemble breadcrumbs.

Transfer to a medium bowl and add the butter and a little salt. Mix to combine and press into the base of the
prepared tin. Refrigerate for 10 minutes or until set.

To make the filling, place the labne, egg yolks, yoghurt and half the sugar in a large bowl and mix well to
combine. Place the egg whites in a clean bowl and whisk, using an electric mixer, until stiff peaks form.
Gradually pour in the remaining sugar, whisking until glossy. In two batches, add the egg white to the labne
mixture and gently fold.

Pour the filling over the base and bake for 45 minutes or until golden. Allow to cool in the tin.

To make the whiskey-honey glaze, melt the honey in a small saucepan over low heat until smooth. Add the
whiskey, lemon juice and salt and stir until combined.

Release the cake from the tin and place on a serving plate or cake stand. Top with the glaze and decorate with
the pecans to serve.

# YOGHURT +
## *chocolate chip* BAKE

*serves* 4

Growing up, my sister Jaime would bake the most delicious natural yoghurt
and chocolate chip muffins – we'd all be crazy for them! This is her recipe
but it's been adapted to make one big share cookie, perfect for breaking
off warm pieces at the table with friends and cups of tea. The yoghurt gives
the bake a soft and almost tangy centre, which is beautiful with the rich
dark chocolate. The challenge is not to eat the whole thing in one go!

*100g butter, chopped and softened*

*1 cup (220g) caster (superfine) sugar*

*2 eggs*

*⅓ cup (80ml) milk*

*1⅓ cups (375g) plain greek-style (thick) yoghurt*

*1 teaspoon vanilla extract*

*2 cups (300g) plain (all-purpose) flour*

*1½ teaspoons baking powder*

*150g dark chocolate chips*

*150g milk chocolate chips*

Preheat oven to 190°C (375°F). Lightly grease a 20cm round
cake tin or baking dish and line with non-stick baking paper.

Place the butter and sugar in a large bowl and beat, using an electric
mixer, until pale and fluffy. Add the eggs, 1 at a time, beating between
each addition. Add the milk, yoghurt and vanilla and mix.

Sift in the flour and baking powder and mix well.
Add the chocolate chips and fold gently to combine.

Pour into the prepared tin and bake for 50 minutes – 1 hour or until firm
and golden. If you notice the top becoming too dark, simply cover
the tin with some aluminium foil for the last 15 minutes of baking time.

Turn the bake out onto a serving plate or board to serve.

# CHERRY and
# macadamia nut BROWNIES

*serves 6–8*

I love to make these fudgy brownies in the winter on a damp and cold day. Candles lit and paired with a steaming cup of tea, it's sure to brighten up your world. The bitter sour cherries give it such a great tang that contrasts with the molten chocolate and crunchy nuts.

*3 eggs*

*½ cup (125g) caster (superfine) sugar*

*225g butter, chopped*

*300g dark chocolate (70% cocoa), chopped*

*100g milk chocolate, chopped*

*⅔ cup (100g) plain (all-purpose) flour*

*25g glacé or dried sour cherries*

*⅓ cup (50g) macadamia nuts, roughly chopped*

Preheat oven to 180°C (350°F). Line 2 x 20cm x 30cm slice tins with non-stick baking paper.

Place the eggs and sugar in a large bowl and beat, using an electric mixer, until pale and thick.

Place the butter and chocolate in a small saucepan over medium heat and stir until melted and smooth. Add to the egg mixture and mix to combine.

Add the flour and fold until smooth. Add the cherries and macadamias and fold.

Divide the mixture between the prepared tins and bake for 35 minutes or until the centres are just firm to the touch.

Allow to cool in the tins for 15 minutes. Turn out onto a wire rack to cool completely or onto a board. Slice into squares and serve warm or cold.

*an edwardian*

**FOODIE**

Aug 11th
1996

52 EATON PLACE,
LONDON, S.W.1.

Brighed, My Glorious Brighed
what a joy to get your call a
few minutes ago, I knew
that when you reconsidered
that you would not take s
a pointless risk with no ben
to anyone and the cause of
incredible anxiety to your fam
and friends: but I am tremen
ously flattered that I helped
you to make your decision

*I*t's 4am. I am sitting by the fire in my cottage reading this, my last letter from Dom, my dear, dear friend, aged 100 and nine months – the ultimate Edwardian.

*52 Eaton Place,*
*London SW1*
*May 15th 1996*

*Dearest Brighid (he never called me Biddy),*

*Irish telephone exchange says it doesn't recognise your number! I am throttled, going to get bottled! Help! Help!*

*Your most ancient rascal,*

*Dom x*

The writing is thin, spidery, a little tipsy. I suspect that it must have taken a great deal of effort to write it. Everyone who knows me knew Dom because any conversations I ever had in those last 12 years were predictably and joyously interrupted by Dom's telephone calls with new recipes and demands to collect yet another case of wine from Mitchell's of Sandycove. In those days I had no idea how unique those wines were and I drank them cheerfully and casually. I had been quaffing Haut Brion and the best Montrachets with sausage rolls on a daily basis.

Age may have trapped Dom in an Edwardian time warp, but it could not trap his heart. Anyone researching the intricacies of refined Edwardian life and food, as I was doing, would have hit the jackpot.

Dom's friendship, his wit and epicurean knowledge has been a huge influence on my life. We wrote to each other once a week (I counted some 1,487 letters I had received). His wicked sense of humour had always left me in stitches and he generously taught me all about the world of traditional French cooking and wine – the likes of Auguste Escoffier, Eugène Herbodeau at the Carlton, François Latry at the Savoy and Marcel Percevault at Claridges.

He was intellectually stimulating, droll and loyal, with a great sense of the ridiculous. He never cooked in his life, but by God, did he love his grub.

*Taillevent, the best restaurant in Paris...*
*Simpsons on the Strand, the best treacle tart and clotted cream...*
*Rules... best Yorkshire pudding, as big as a pillow, Dear...*
*Florence, we must all go all there...*
*Rice pudding... it has to be the Connaught.*

I was first introduced to Dom, (*Lord Oranmore and Browne* as he was formally known), on a windy day, his birthday, in London many years earlier by his son.

I was a working journalist in those days, one who had taken a dim view of many of the Anglo-Irish I had met and interviewed.

In my opinion, the Anglo-Irish were a strange breed. I had witnessed outrageous behaviour first hand and I couldn't believe that they acted out disgracefully 'knowing' that they were being interviewed. The majority of them had 'servants' called 'Brigid', or 'Bridie' and all had empty fridges full of mildew. To me they were an ignorant people, neither Irish nor English, utterly arrogant and demeaning in their treatment of Irish country people. They surrounded themselves at hunt balls with their cronies, fawning parasites, broke Maharajah, racing bums, wasters and penniless earls. Their Irish 'servants', decent country people, had to pay the price, working long hours for pitiful wages and often abuse. There were some exceptions, of course – the Leslies of Castle Leslie, Lord Kilbracken and Dom – among them.

Despite been born Anglo-Irish and living a life of enviable luxury, he had none of their traits – he was salty and true and he was the mightiest friend in the world. I was simply spellbound by his stories of Edwardian life.

He remembered being forced to swallow tablespoons of treacle and sulphur as an Edwardian child; wearing a belt of soft red 'Swan cloth' from the Aran Islands to keep his kidneys warm; loving heroin during an operation in 1920; and dinner at the Derby.

"We had a splendid birthday lunch at Claridges," he said that day, holding his wife Sally's hand (1930s screen starlet, *Miss Sally Gray*) and slumping back into the sofa opposite me. He pressed a big brass bell beside his chair. Within seconds, a bottle of Haut Brion was presented by his home help, Dolores.

"Cheers to eejits great and small," said Dom as he drained a glass. Drinks were served with bread and small flat cylinders of Bonchester cheese in the drawing room. The cheese was divine, at once punchy and pungent, "only the best for Brighid!!," he said fanning himself with a large white ostrich fan that once belonged to Gaby Deslys, the Marilyn Monroe of 1920's Paris.

Inside the elegant room we three feasted, tucking into 'takeaway' from the Roux Brothers. It was superb and Dom's favourite was "Le Caneton Gavroche". (It's the entire duck poached in consommé and served with three sauces). At the same time, delicate little cardboard boxes were opened to reveal crab in aspic and lobster with Aquitaine sauce. It was all a revelation to me as I chomped away and took detailed notes, making a promise to myself to check out the recipes.

There was no doubt about it, Dom had led a charmed, indulgent life beginning in Castlemacgarrett, County Mayo, Dublin and later London. Old newspaper photographs showed him with every conceivable literary and political figure of the time – the Duke and Duchess of Windsor, Emperor Hirohito and Lord Lucan.

The following day, at 1pm, the delightfully urbane Dom and Sally made a regal entrance into Wilton's at 55 Jermyn Street (famous for its game. It is the bastion of British cuisine). He was dressed in a cashmere Crombie with white and tan correspondent shoes and Sally wore the most amazing navy felt hat. The restaurant was very stuffy, even stiff.

"Wilton's once existed as an oyster stall in1742," said Dom. "My ancestors ate here. They serve the best oysters, fish and game." He ordered two dozen Beau Brummell oysters, black sole and a bottle of Chateau Montrachet. I knew nothing about wine but I was learning fast.

*October 20th 1997*
*Eaton Square,*
*London,*

*Dearest Brighid,*

*I'm so thrilled about my birthday trip to Paris!! It is worth being 98 years old! It will be smashing. Oops, my osteopath has just arrived. He is looking hungry so must rush and lock up all your delicious goodies. (Homemade gingerbread, a fruitcake and smoked salmon which I had carried all the way to London.)*

*Yesterday, a jeroboam of Chateau Mouton Rothschild Claret 1945 fetched £71,000 in Christies. That is equal to £1,702 a glass or £243 a sip. Financially, I think I've finished quite a lot of it since 1901. I used to drink it regularly in Castlemagarrett, when I lived in Mayo. I think it was about 4 pounds a bottle!!*

*You must be getting fed up with all the Edwardian recipes I keep sending you but as your champion and researcher-in-chief, I feel it is my job. I talked to Garech yesterday (Dom's son). He is looking forward to the birthday trip and he says he will get us all rooms in Paris. Perhaps you could be indulgent and spend four days in Paris with Sally, Garech and I?*

*Your old but loving rascal,*

*Dom.*

I couldn't wait to go.

"Golly," said Sally, as we pulled out of Victoria Station en route to Paris – "I heard something pop, I think it's a champagne bottle." "Sally knows her onions," laughed Dom, sitting snug as a bug in his camel haired Inverlochy, an old-fashioned coat used solely for train travel. We were all so excited as the train ploughed its way to Paris to celebrate Dom's 98th birthday.

"Champagne, Madame," said the waiter in French. "Mais oui," said Sally dangling her glass. She gulped it down in seconds. He returned several minutes later with the wine list. "Montagney or Chablis Saint Martin,?" "Mais oui, Chablis," said Sally.

Between courses, Dom presented me with a bulky envelope bursting with newspaper cuttings, and articles he had kept for me on cookery and wine. It had clearly been full time work and I was touched. Each cutting had to be carefully unfolded, passed to me, read by me, accepted or rejected by me or returned to the envelope for future inspection. One of his notes described roasted bone marrow. I balked. "Oh, don't frown dear Brighid, roasted bone marrow was once a dish of great fashion. When I was a young man, one of our favourite savouries was bone marrow. The servants served the bones in warm white napkins and we used a long silver spoon to extract the marrow. Delicious. It was eaten after pudding." (I later realised this was a peculiarly Edwardian English habit of serving something savoury as the final course. It was designed to show off one's servants and one's silver in the old days of the English Empire). It sounded a tad disgusting but was obviously incredibly nutritious. It's ironic, considering that currently, foodies are resorting to bowls of bone broth as a healthy option on menus. Yet bone broth was the norm in Edwardian times. Who knew?

## PARIS

At Gare Du Nord, a waiting car whisked us to Hotel De La Tremoille. Both Sally and Dom surrendered their faces to the joyful moment that, once again, at ages 98 and 88 they had made it to Paris. It gave me the deepest pleasure to see their happiness.

## HOTEL RESTAURANT

"Alors," said Dom, peering at the menu. "I shall have 'perdreau roti entier aux marons,'(partridge stuffed with chesnuts) and Sally and Brighid would like sele d'agneau farcie l'estragon" (saddle of lamb with tarragon.)

## RESTAURANT TAILLEVENT

The next morning, Dom's birthday, in room 408, I unwrapped the birthday cake I had baked in Dublin. A foot-high madeira cherry cake. His favourite. Dom was thrilled. He opened the picture I drew of him and hugged me.

"Brighid, we are off to somewhere special, said Dom. "Is it 'Le Voltaire?' Or is it perhaps L'Ami Louis?", he teased.

"Taillevent!" said Sally.

"Aha, Taillevent," said Dom, "where the chef cooks exactly as the chefs once cooked for Louis XV. Did you know that King Louis was partial to Lievre a la Royal, a dish made with hare and port wine," said Dom beginning to chuckle. "But because he had lost all his teeth, the chef had to make the hare very soft to be able to eat it so he stuffed it with foie gras." "Didn't he have syphilis, Darling... and didn't his toes fall off in his shoes?" quizzed Sally. "Yes Darling, but he didn't eat with his feet." We all laughed.

Dom scanned the wine list. 75,000 bottles of wine was perhaps even too much for him. "Two bottles of Chateau Figeac 1986 and two bottles of Lavelle Haut Brion," said Dom.

I am happy to report that the Lievre a la Royal was rich and gamey, a la Louis.

Two hours later, the waiter appeared with a shiny chocolate cake for Dom with Bon Anniversaire 1901 on it and we started all over again.

"I've no sense of direction," said Sally, shuffling towards le toillette, "because I have no sense."

## RESTAURANT VOLTAIRE – THE FOLLOWING DAY

Jimmy Douglas, a rich American ex-pat who once had an infamous romance with Woolworths heiress, Barbara Hutton, had lived in Paris for 45 years and was waiting for us at the bar. Jimmy was full of stories and intrigue. The Voltaire was noisy and lively. "Brighid, as a gourmand, you must order 'Quenelles de brochet', a famous Parisian dish made from creamed pike," said Jimmy.

I overheard Jimmy Douglas asking Dom his favourite three things in life. "The three things I like best have been the three W's – women, wine and woodcocks. If I was asked to come back again, I'd say the same." Jimmy roared with laughter.

## BACK HOME

I shall never forget Dom and Sally and our petite voyage. Two sweeter, kinder and wittier people would be hard to find.

The last time I saw Dom and Sally together was at lunch in the Cadogan Hotel in London. Dom was drinking champagne through a straw. He joked about death, "cycling to heaven."

Later that evening I was asleep in my hotel room when the telephone rang. It was Dom, in tears. "I rang to say goodbye," he said. I told him I wasn't leaving until the following day. Armed with a bunch of blue Delphiniums for Sally and a marshmallow clown for Dom, I marched to Eaton Place and pressed the bell. "I'm going, going, going!" he cried.

"Going where? I asked.

"Going to die."

"Never," I said.

But tears streamed down his face. "You'll have to face it Darling, I shall be off cycling any time now. Please God I shall see you soon Brighid."

"God shall be very pleased," I said

I received a phone call that he had cycled off on me one rainy afternoon in the cottage. It was Dom's housekeeper Sammy. She floored me with the news. "I am so sorry Brighid, 'Lordy' has passed away just now."

I simply couldn't believe it.

Frankly, my life has never been the same since the days of Dom and Sally. Arranged in front of me are photographs of them. His wonderful letters, gathering dust, and recipes like a sequence of dreams, memories and episodes from the magical world of my Edwardian friend.

# DRINKS

*marmalade* WHISKEY SOUR

*serves* 2

I must admit I don't particularly like whiskey, so it's strange that my favourite cocktail is a whiskey sour. Then again, as my Nan likes to say fondly, I'm "as odd as two left shoes." Usually, you need to make a simple sugar syrup for these, but a teaspoonful of marmalade does the trick, bringing its lovely orange flavour.

*ice cubes, for shaking, plus extra to serve (optional)*

*2 teaspoons orange marmalade*

*¼ cup (60ml) jameson whiskey*

*¼ cup (60ml) lemon juice*

*1½ tablespoons egg white*

*angostura bitters, to serve*

*lemon slices, to serve*

*finely grated orange rind, to serve*

Place the ice, marmalade, whiskey, lemon juice and egg white in a cocktail shaker and shake until combined and chilled.

Divide between serving glasses over ice and top each with a few drops of bitters, a slice of lemon and some orange rind, to serve.

*elderflower*

# GRAPE SMASH

*serves* 2

I learnt this recipe years ago, when working in restaurants, and I've held onto it ever since – it's so refreshing and I love the unusual use of grapes. Their sweetness and colour make the perfect tart, summery drink. I'll often multiply the quantities and make a big jug for when I have friends over.

¾ *cup (100g) seedless red grapes (about 20 grapes)*

⅓ *cup (80ml) vodka*

*2 tablespoons elderflower cordial or water*

¼ *cup (60ml) white grape juice*

*ice cubes, to serve*

*soda water, to serve*

Place the grapes in a jug and, using a muddler or wooden spoon, roughly mash them. Add the vodka, cordial and grape juice and mix to combine.

Divide between serving glasses over ice and top with soda water to serve.

# GINGER + LEMONGRASS *root tea*

*serves 2*

On a recent yoga trip to Bali I became totally enamoured with this soothing tea. The Balinese use nothing but fresh ingredients, and you can really taste how nourishing it is. It simultaneously perks you up and calms the nervous system. The smell alone as you sip this is truly divine.

*2 stalks lemongrass*

*5cm piece ginger*

*1 lime*

*2 cups (500ml) freshly boiled water*

*2 teaspoons honey*

*lemon peel, to garnish*

*mint leaves, to garnish*

Wash the lemongrass stalks, peel away the outer leaves and trim the darker green top. Using the back of a large knife, bruise the white part. Peel the ginger and bruise it in the same way.

Halve the lime and squeeze the juice into serving glasses. Add the lemongrass and ginger and top with the water. Allow to steep for 5 minutes. Add the honey and stir to combine. Garnish with the lemon peel and mint leaves to serve.

# *the grapevine's* GOOSEBERRY + ELDERFLOWER *cocktail*

*serves* 6–10

The Grapevine wine bar in Dalkey is one of my favourite haunts. They serve
a summer cocktail of gooseberries and elderflower with prosecco that is
fragrant and delicious. The sweet scented white blossom of the elderflower
is unforgettable. In winter, when the gooseberries are out of season, they serve
a Christmas version of elderflower and prosecco with floating cranberries,
which is just as fresh and fabulous. This recipe makes plenty of cordial
so it's great to make ahead before entertaining.

*¼ cups (62ml) water*

*¼ cup (55g) caster (superfine) sugar*

*2¾ cups (550g) gooseberries, trimmed*

*4 small stems elderflower*

*chilled prosecco, to serve*

Place the water and sugar in a medium heavy-based saucepan over
medium heat and cook, stirring occasionally, until the sugar dissolves. Cook
for a further 2–3 minutes or until slightly thick, then add the gooseberries.
Cook until the skins break, then remove the pan from the heat.

Shake the elderflower stems to remove any dirt or small insects
(washing will reduce the flavour) and add to the pan. Stir to combine
and allow the cordial to cool and infuse overnight.

Drain the cordial through a sieve lined with muslin and pour
into a sterilised jar or bottle.

To serve, place 30ml of the cordial into each champagne flute,
plus a gooseberry, and top with prosecco.

# CHRISTMAS

# BOURBON + *salted* *maple butter* ROAST TURKEY

*serves* 4–5

The marriage of salty and sweet is one that shouldn't work for roasted turkey, but magically it does. Salt is a flavour enhancer, so if you mix salt and syrup together, the salt enhances the sweetness not only of the syrup but the turkey meat itself. As for the dark amber richness of boozy bourbon? What can I say? Utterly delicious.

*1 x 5kg whole organic or free-range turkey,*
*neck and giblets removed, at room temperature*

*270g butter, chopped*

*½ cup (125ml) maple syrup*

*½ cup (125ml) bourbon whiskey*

*sea salt flakes, to taste*

Preheat oven to 180°C (350°F). Rinse the turkey under cold water. Using paper towel, pat both the inside and outside of the turkey dry. Place the turkey on a lightly greased rack set over a large roasting pan.

Place the butter in a medium saucepan over medium heat. Add the maple, bourbon and a pinch of salt and stir to combine until melted and smooth. Allow to cool a little.

Working from the neck of the turkey, carefully push your hands under the skin to separate it from the flesh, until you reach the end of the breast. Rub three-quarters of the butter mixture under the skin. Baste the entire turkey with the remaining butter mixture.

Cover the turkey loosely with non-stick baking paper and place in the middle of the oven. Roast for 2 hours, basting every 20 minutes. Remove the baking paper and roast for a further 1 hour 30 minutes or until golden and cooked through (the juices should run clear when the thickest part of the thigh is pierced).

Cover with aluminium foil and allow to rest for 20 minutes before serving.

# crispy BACON
# roasted PARTRIDGES

*serves* 4

One of the best meals I've ever eaten, was the simplest. One hot Majorcan day, my sister Siobhan and I were invited to the Mayor of Soller, Don Pedro A. Serra's home for lunch. I was hugely excited, as the Mayor had been a friend of the artist Miro and had written a book about his life. When we arrived, there were about twenty family members seated outside. A large wooden table was set up under the shade of some orange trees. Outside, I noticed an oven built into the wall of their home. Local Majorcan women in aprons were busy cooking. The smoky smell was intense and I was both hungry and intrigued. Eventually, lunch was served, a tray of crispy skinned roasted partridges, accompanied by another tray of gigantic roasted peaches drizzled with honey and rosemary. The partridge's creamy, gently-cooked meat had a buttery flavour and tasted less-gamey than snipe, pheasant or woodcock. The combination of peach and partridge was exquisite. It was the finest dinner. Ever since I have loved partridge, especially in September when it is in season.

*4 x 375g partridges, trimmed and giblets removed*

*80g butter, softened*

*4 sage leaves*

*8 rashers smoked streaky bacon (90g)*

*sea salt & cracked black pepper, to taste*

Preheat oven to 220°C (425°F). Lightly grease a large roasting pan or casserole dish.

Using paper towel, pat both the inside and outside of the partridges dry. Rub half the butter over their skins and spoon the remaining butter into the cavities.

Arrange the partridges, breast side up, in the prepared pan and top with a sage leaf. Drape each partridge with 2 slices of bacon (this adds salty goodness and helps to retain moisture). Season with a little salt and pepper and roast for 20–30 minutes or until cooked through, golden and the bacon is crispy. Serve with crunchy stuffing (see *recipe*, page 262), if you like.

*nora's*

# CHRISTMAS PUDDINGS

*makes* 1 large pudding and
1 small pudding

My fiancé's grandmother, Nora, was an extraordinary woman. She raised
a family of three children by herself, after being widowed at a young age.
She worked full-time and was also an incredible cook! Of course, she kept
a detailed journal, packed to the brim with recipes, in her careful, delicate
handwriting. I felt very privileged to be given this piece of history when
starting our project. With gems like this delicious Christmas pudding, I'm
honoured that I can continue a small part of her legacy by cooking and
sharing beautiful recipes. I hope you enjoy one of my favourites of hers.

¾ cup (110g) plain (all-purpose) flour

1 cup (120g) almond meal (ground almonds)

1 teaspoon sea salt flakes

2 teaspoons mixed spice

½ teaspoon ground cinnamon

½ teaspoon ground nutmeg

450g beef or vegetarian suet, finely chopped

6½ cups (450g) breadcrumbs

2½ cups (440g) brown sugar

3 cups (450g) each raisins, sultanas and currants

½ cup (110g) glacé cherries

1½ cups (110g) candied peel

⅔ cup (110g) almonds, halved

1 large apple, peeled and grated

1 large carrot, peeled and grated

8 eggs

½ cup (125ml) stout

lemon juice, to taste

Preheat oven to 150°C (300°F). Lightly grease 1 x 4-cup-capacity (1-litre) pudding bowl and
1 x 10-cup-capacity (2.5-litre) pudding bowl (both with lids).

Sift the flour, almond meal, salt and the spices into a large bowl. Add the suet and breadcrumbs and mix
well. Add the sugar, fruit, peel, almonds, apple and carrot and combine.

Place the eggs in a separate large bowl and whisk until thick and creamy. Add the stout and beat until just
combined. Add the egg mixture to the fruit mixture and mix well. Add the lemon juice and mix.

Rinse 2 large squares of clean muslin under boiling water. Allow to cool a little, squeeze dry and spread
onto a clean surface. Dust the damp muslins lightly with extra flour and use them to line the pudding bowls.
Divide the pudding mixture between the bowls and press so it fits snugly. Bring together the muslin and tie with
kitchen string to secure. Clip the lids onto the bowls. Wrap the bowls in a layer each of non-stick baking paper
and aluminium foil. Place the bowls in a large roasting pan or baking dish and fill it half-full with boiling water
(about 5cm deep). Cover the entire tray with a double layer of aluminium foil. Bake for 5 hours, replenishing
the boiling water in the pan every 1 hour. Allow the puddings to cool in the bowls, then unwrap and turn
them out onto serving plates.

Serve immediately or cover with baking paper and return to the bowls. Cover bowls with aluminium foil or 2
layers of plastic wrap and store in a cool dark place for up to 1 month. Re-steam to serve.

*crunchy herb*

# + FRUIT STUFFING

*serves 4—6*

Stuffing is a matter of personal taste. Some like it cooked inside the bird.
I, myself, loathe it this way. I have too many bad memories of congealed,
grey, lumpy stuffing! This recipe I created is really simple to make, suitable
for vegetarians and is super tasty, with a lovely crunchy texture.
I use ordinary sliced white bread from the supermarket for this mix, as it
makes for a more golden, crispy texture. Serve it alongside roasted
turkey, chicken, pork or partridge.

300g sliced white bread (about 6–7 slices), torn into pieces

200g butter, chopped

1 medium onion, finely chopped

3 green onions (scallions), trimmed and finely chopped

1 large bulb (head) garlic, chopped

½ cup (55g) chopped walnuts

½ cup (75g) chopped dried apricots

2 tablespoons finely chopped tarragon leaves

½ cup finely chopped flat-leaf parsley leaves

1 teaspoon finely chopped sage leaves

1 tablespoon thyme leaves

1 teaspoon dried thyme leaves

sea salt flakes, to taste

cracked black, white and pink pepper (optional), to taste

finely grated rind of 1 lemon

finely grated rind of 1 orange

Preheat oven to 180°C (350°F). Process the bread, in batches, into coarse crumbs.

Melt the butter in a large non-stick frying pan over medium heat. Add the onion, green
onions and garlic and cook, stirring, for 5 minutes or until softened. Add the walnuts and
apricots and cook, stirring, for 3 minutes or until just beginning to brown.

Add the breadcrumbs, herbs, salt, pepper and citrus rinds and toss to combine.

Transfer the mixture to a large roasting pan and roast for 30 minutes, stirring regularly,
until crunchy and golden brown.

THANK YOU!

**B**The first thanks goes to Críostóir MacCárthaigh, Patricia, Jonny and all the great people who work in the Department of Folklore, U.C.D. Your help is greatly appreciated. Equally generous with their knowledge and expertise have been Mr. Pat Henchy, with his insights into Irish culinary history; James, Margaret and Tommy Connolly, Moycullen, County Galway; Tom and Padraic Walsh, Ugool Mountain, Moycullen; Mr. David Went, Margaret and Fionbarr Farrell and Kathleen, Coliemore Road, Dalkey. Thank you also to our chief tasters, Mr. Ken Cunningham, the ferry man, Mr. Pat Dalton and Mr. Shay Kennedy.

Bill O'Dea, mycologist, thank you. Kady and I had great craic with Michael Masterson, Mark Nicholl and 'the Deputy' in Longford. A huge thank you. I owe everything to my wonderful friends and family;

Anne and Nell Fitzgerald, the finest pastry makers in Dublin. My wonderful sister Aisling Mc Laughlin for her extraordinary editing skills, patience and kindness. To my dear friends, Geraldine Walsh, of the Dublin Civic Trust, Margaret O'Callaghan aka 'Magsieboo', Don O'Callaghan, Finula Keane aka 'Maisie'. Thank you Mr. Denis O'Connell for your unstinting enthusiasm, wit and generosity. To the wonderful Mr. Graham O'Donnell land his partner Maeve Nunan for all their enthusiasm. Others who should also be mentioned include:

Mr. Peter Fallon, Gallery Press for permission to include my late friend Michael Hartnett's poignant poem, 'Mo Ghrá Thú'. Cormac Bourke; the Sunday Independent, Dublin for permission to publish extracts from interviews published in this newspaper.

A big thank you to all the Dalkey restaurants and hostelries who have helped us relax after long months of hard work. Tony Weir, Jason, Conor and Sarah, The Kings Inn, Dalkey. Gabriel, Pam, John Hoard, Carol Cunningham, Graham and Nicky, The Grapevine Wine Bar, Dalkey. Donal Hick and Martin of Hick's butchers, Dalkey, shared their wonderful butchering expertise and culinary secrets with me when I snuck in to the back of the shop. Thank you Gary and Omar, The Dalkey Duck; Mervyn Stewart, chef and owner of the legendary Guinea Pig Restaurant, Dalkey; Cavistons fish mongers, Glasthule; Noel Kavanagh, Butcher, Glasthule; Doyle's Butcher's, Castle Street. And, of course, my buddy, Kady, who has spent the most time with me, travelling, cooking, tasting, laughing.

Finally, I dedicate my section of this book to my late sister Siobhan 'Seanie' McLaughlin, my chef, mentor and beloved sister and my darling son, Johnny.

**K**This cookbook has been a dream come true. I have always wanted to write a cookbook that I could also design and photograph – this has been an incredible journey. I have learned so much along the way and have so many people to thank. They've made it what it is. This book is dedicated to my fiancé and best friend Niall. I have no idea how someone can have as much patience as you do. You have been there to taste, edit, clean up, read, correct and help with every stage of this book. You are the most supportive partner I could ever ask for and I am so thankful to have you by my side, I love you! x

To my Dad, Denis, thank you for always believing in me and being so supportive of the book, ever since it was a tiny seed of an idea.

To my Nan, Carrie, thank you for always being there for me, with a joke or smile, cups of tea and the cosiest fire in all of Ireland.

To our editor, Abby Pfahl, you have been incredible and the book would not be the same without you. Thank you for your guidance and incredible eye. Tal Gilead and Kip Carrol, you have been amazing. To Scott Fairweather, I cannot thank you enough for your support and look forward to shooting with you. Eamon Eastwood, from Taste Ireland, thank you for always being so supportive and including me in the Taste family.

Thank you to the Gilhoolys, Trudi, Berleena and Philip for sharing your amazing stories and recipes. My family, who is always so supportive. A special thanks to Tori for her photography skills and helping me pick photos to use. It has been so great to have you in Sydney. Jaime for your recipe and food inspo and being a great sounding board for all my ideas!

Thanks to all of my wonderful friends, Jenny, Dervla, Gemma, Clara, Sue, Berleena and everyone that has made me feel so at home in Sydney. You may not have realised, but even checking in and asking how the book is going has helped keep me focused!

Thank you Biddy for starting this crazy adventure with me. Who knew when we first met it would lead to trips all around Ireland and then Sydney and Italy. I have thoroughly enjoyed embracing my true 'muck savage' wining and dining with you!

Finally to all my friends and colleagues that are so supportive of my ventures, from Kady's Kitchen to pop-up restaurants, I feel so lucky to have you all in my corner. I hope our readers enjoy this book as much as we have enjoyed creating it. Love, Kady xx

## AUTHORS' NOTES

A note on measuring – this book is universal, and while there is very little difference between Australian and European cup measures (and most recipes are not affected by this), all the recipes have been created using Australian measurements. So, if you'd like to be super precise:

> 1 Australian teaspoon holds 5ml
> 1 Australian tablespoon holds 20ml
> 1 Australian cup holds 250ml

All cup and spoon measures are level, unless stated otherwise.
We have used fan-forced ovens, so as a general rule, you will need to increase the temperature slightly if you are using a conventional oven.

Recipe writing and compilation – Brighid 'Biddy' McLaughlin and Kady O Connell
Story writing – Brighid 'Biddy' McLaughlin

Art direction and design – Kady Creative

Food photography and styling – Kady's Kitchen
Lifestyle photography – Kady's Kitchen | Copyright © Kady Creative 2017
Photography page 3 – Anthony Woods | Copyright © Anthony Woods 2017
Photography page 5 – Tal Gilead | Copyright © Tal Gilead 2017
Food Photography page 173 – Annie Spratt | Copyright © Annie Spratt 2017 (unsplash.com)
Food Photography page 211 – Hanny Naibaho | Copyright © Hanny Naibaho 2017 (unsplash.com)
Cover photography, introduction page and pages 175; 187; 188; 209; 251; 252; 255; 256; 259; 260; 263 – Kip Carrol | Copyright © Kip Carrol 2017
Photography editing – Kady Creative; Tal Gilead

Copy and recipe editing – Abby Pfahl
Story editing – Aisling McLaughlin
Indexing – Kit Carstairs

First published October 2017
Kady Creative
Bondi, NSW, 2026, Australia
kady@kadycreative.com
kadycreative.com
 @kadycreative

For more recipes and food inspiration, visit **kadyskitchen.com**
 kadyskitchen_   /kadyskitchen

and **Biddys Cottage**
 /biddyscottage  e  biddymclaughlin@gmail.com